Domain 2- *Managing Learners for Learning*

Power of Teaching—*the Science of the Art*

Behavioral Pathway to **Teaching** Excellence
In Grades PreK-14

Dr. Joseph Wise

&

David Sundstrom, J.D

Cataloguing Data:
    ISBN 978-0-9841197-0-7
    Wise, Joseph
    Sundstrom, David
        Power of Teaching—the Science of the Art
        Behavioral Pathway to **Teaching** Excellence in Grades PreK-14

      1.   Education 2. Teaching 3. Classroom Pedagogy
           Acquiring Editor: David Sundstrom
           Production Editor: Victor Frush
Printed in the United States of America
Copyright © January 20, 2008; November 25, 2009; January 12, 2010

Power of Teaching- The Science of the Art

Contents

Domain 1- *Focusing & Engaging Minds*

Important Acknowledgements

Numerous and important colleagues and trusted advisors have contributed mightily with their valued editing and practitioner expertise. Among them is my longest-term associate and teacher in this work: Dr. Amy Brown, who since 1976 inspired me with the drive to become a teacher, and the stamina to become a teacher and lifelong learner.

Other important advisors include Drs. Eric Smith, Brenda Tanner, Michael Walls, Susan Purser, Shawn Smith, Lloyd Martin and Bart Anderson. Others who lent valuable technical advisement include Matt Chapman, Pat Deck, Victor Frush, Ginger Hopkins, Jim Huge, Tom McDowell, Debby Raper, and Bill Slotnik.

Thank you too, to whom some would say is my most-indispensible associate in this work: David Sundstrom. David has been my trusted advisor, trusted confidante, trusted principal- and principled-assistant in all of my work of the past decade. For *Power of Teaching*, David has served as chief editor with tireless patience, perseverance and professionalism.

Power of Teaching began as a research endeavor in 2002 so that I could better assist my colleagues in powering-up the work in their classrooms. In 2007, David joined the project and assumed the role of chief editor, to ensure the research connects to practitioners with a high degree of relevance. In 2009, Victor Frush joined the project to format this second edition. Both have added aptly to the usefulness of the work and I am deeply appreciative of their contributions.

To the many, many teachers and instructional leaders I know who work tirelessly and in the great spirit of continuous improvement, to make their practice better and better, thank you for your commitment to our children, each and every day.

Joseph Wise

Notes:

Introduction

Remarkable transformations have taken place over the past 30 years in preK-12 educational systems, particularly in public schools. Many of these changes have enriched schools and school systems by creating systemic improvements; many have additionally heightened our awareness of what effective teaching of children actually involves. Some transformative actions, however, have been devastating. Adoption and implementation of these more destructive initiatives have weakened the work being done in preK-12 classrooms, and set in motion certain practices and protocols that undermine daily instruction.

Over a period of decades and despite the more recent posturing around *No Child Left Behind,* we have blurred an essential component of our work—Accountability. Gone is the era in which Madeline Hunter and other scholars were working to help us develop our teaching skills, behavior management skills, and greater depth and understanding of the subjects we were teaching. I recall learning about accountability in the work of Bennett Reimer and Bernard Dubroski at Northwestern University. I recall their hope and prediction that a movement was afoot—a movement that would cause greater focus on meeting the needs of each and every child, including those who didn't shine with obvious gifts.

I remember also being deeply and fittingly influenced by the powerful education practices of Amy Brown, Clifford Madsen, and other education leaders at Florida State University. Each spoke of Accountability, and of challenging ourselves and our students to become academically, artistically, culturally, and socially stronger than any previous generation. Accountability, at its essence, is not a goal; it is the acceptance of responsibility for all that we do in our classrooms, day in and day out. It is a commitment to continuous examination, reflection and improvement.

Many of those who entered education as a profession when I did knew the upside of Accountability; all of us were confident we would personally make a difference. What we weren't prepared to manage, however, was a coming downside of Accountability; a competing philosophy that was beginning to look back at regimented instruction with a sanitized fondness. It was nostalgia really, for a world that had never felt the need—or desire—to acknowledge the multiple ways in which children learn. Or the multiple ways in which they fail to learn when simple "chalk 'n talk" instruction is all that is provided in the classroom. Before we knew it, educators nationwide were focusing wholly on the *what* of teaching—without effectively confronting the far messier (but pivotal) *how* of teaching.

No doubt, the *what* is an essential component of teaching. But we don't teach in a vacuum. And it is evident that teaching centered solely on the *content* of what is being taught—while ignoring the *how* of delivering that content effectively—is deadly. The practice enables us to reach only a fraction of students in public school classrooms, and ignores a fundamental reality: Our students continue to learn in diverse and different ways often despite our well-intentioned efforts. The bottom line for us now is that Accountability for only the *what* of everything that is being taught and tested is not enough. If we are to make sustainable change in the lives of our students through education, we as educators must establish accountability for the *how* of teaching.

The current education accountability movement began, at least in spirit through politics, in 1983, following the disturbing findings documented in *A Nation at Risk: The Imperative For Educational Reform*. Initially, Congress enacted several versions of school reforms, culminating in the now-famous and strongly debated *No Child Left Behind* (NCLB) legislation. NCLB, with the rules and regulations promulgated under it, comprises more than 700 pages; it was, at the time of its passage into law, the most far-reaching and the most compelling bi-partisan effort toward educational reform in US history. For the first time, communities were required to disclose for public examination not just *aggregated* data on their schools, but also *disaggregated* data that revealed startling—and disturbing— disparity among students. We as a nation were compelled to confront something that had long been vaguely apparent but unacknowledged: Most of our children in poverty, our children of color, our children with disabilities, and our children of foreign born parents were performing at unacceptably deficient academic levels. Their academic performance had been, for years, concealed by aggregated data that implied *all* students at a school to have been doing fine (because most students in that school were doing just fine). Children who did not form a majority at their schools, simply put, were being literally left behind. Few educators or parents seemed to be noticing or troubled by it.

No Child Left Behind mandates that *all* children in *all* schools shall no longer be "left behind" by the year 2014. Although **Power of Teaching** was first introduced long before NCLB, it shares one essential goal with the Act: making the work we do in classrooms more effective. **Power of Teaching** recognizes that we have not been doing enough of the right things to effectively support the work of our teachers and their students. Continued exploitation of preK-12 education as a platform for those who are politically ambitious, vulnerable, or agenda-driven dominates the landscape, and disproportionately impairs meaningful efforts at change. *Accountability* has become the buzz word that resonates with parents and politicians who like their measurements easy to calculate. *What* gets taught is easy to track; content is tangible and quantifiable. *How* content gets taught—and the effectiveness of teaching strategies and behaviors—are far more difficult to measure, and to analyze.

This focus on the *what* has led us to multiple state and local debates concerning *what* academic standards are adopted, *what* assessments are valid and used, *what* curriculum is implemented, *what* data are analyzed, *what* policies are embraced—and ultimately, *what* information we present to our children. This one-dimensional approach to teaching and learning measures only a part of the equation by focusing on *content*—a potent political and policy issue—in isolation from all else. But deciding on and measuring only *what* is taught manifests a constant churn, and continues to conceal a fundamental flaw in the work we do.

We now discount or wholly ignore the *how* of teaching and *how* of learning. We measure and re-measure and measure again AYP—each state's and each school's <u>A</u>dequate <u>Y</u>early <u>P</u>rogress that is mandated federally but implemented in more than 50 separate ways. We engage in benchmark testing, high stakes testing, measurement of student population and population trends, measurement of students-per-class and students-per-employee; measurement of the number of impoverished students and number of racially-identifiable students per school or district; measurement of special education services offered— and the *what* measurement lists go on. It is not that our work on the *what* of teaching is entirely without merit; it is clear, however, that this narrow-minded focus on the *what* is not enough. It never has been.

No Child Left Behind has had some positive effects on our culture, and on the way we educate our children. Those positive effects remain outweighed, however, by the tremendous design flaws inherent within NCLB. Despite the avowed intent of the Act, certain inherent inequities in education—that were acknowledged 30, 50, and even 80 years ago—remain intact in the United States. Part of this is rooted in an indefensible argument that—as a matter of constitutional "states' rights"—each state may customize academic standards to varying and often provincial extremes. New and rewritten laws flow freely from federal, state, and even local politicians in the form of E.S.E.A, I.D.E.A., A.D.A., Section 504, and so on. The legislative mandates grow and undulate, without cohesion and without genuine effectiveness.

The more these scantily funded (or wholly unfunded) mandates flow, without better and more direct investments in our teachers' core work, the more we as a nation will continue to miss the mark. Early work of the Obama administration has made many hopeful that NCLB and federal funding deficiencies are on course for correction. The bold leadership appearing now at the federal level, however, must be matched at the district and school levels. And a renewed focus on teaching practice must be a part of it all.

Without a focus on our practices in the classroom, nations with which we compete will continue to stand back in wonder as low-standards/low-expectation-states con-tinue to brag that their students and schools have made AYP while their children graduate without mastering Algebra or even becoming fully literate. AYP—the elastic measure of academic achievement that states are currently allowed to jury-rig to meet local political needs—continues at this time to be largely misleading and meaningless. Under *No Child Left Behind,* the standard by which we hold students and educators accountable is illusory because it has no consistent definition. Compare low-expectations states with places like Missouri and South Carolina; states reeling from low AYP achievers because their expectations are so high. Such a gross variation among state standards results in us comparing apples to oranges and oranges to vegetables. If the goal is to improve educational practices. The bottom line is this: inconsistent AYP standards do *nothing* to prepare our students for the world they are currently in—and in which they will be compelled

to compete. The arguments and political debates over just what levels should be considered "at-standard" will continue unabated if we as a nation continue to delegate—to state and local units of government—the very standards by which *all* of our children will be ultimately measured.

Power of Teaching does not pretend that thoughtful leadership on the *how* of teaching is entirely absent from our preK-12 and college teaching profession. However, much of the leadership provided on *how* teachers teach has been narrowly focused, disjointed, and flat-out misguiding. For us to effectively lead and support our teachers, we must provide constructive, holistic, and behaviorally measureable guidance on *how* to engage students in the content being taught. By supporting and guiding teachers in the way instruction is delivered, classroom teaching will not be simply correlative to learning. It will be causal.

Historically intense focus on the *what* of teaching has led us away from a healthy balance of all that goes into true academic achievement. *How* we teach, *how* we challenge, *how* we redirect, and *how* we engage students is of no less importance than the *what* of all we profess to teach. Ironically, over the years we actually have learned much and documented much about best practices in education. The literature demonstrates that we already have explored and analyzed much about the *how* of teaching; we simply haven't acknowledged its pivotal effect on academic growth.

Regardless of whether you support the vision behind NCLB or the Accountability movement as each has progressed, it is now up to us, and our entire generation of educators and educational leaders, to ensure that the work in every classroom, every day, is powerful. And powerful teaching is as much about *communication* as it is about the content communicated.

With this work and **Power of Teaching** comes my hope that every teacher—and every educational leader—can take to heart what each has to offer. There is so much we can do. And so much we must do.

Joseph Wise

Notes:

Notes:

Chapter One
What Do Kids Know?

Give your students as much responsibility for their learning as possible.

--Carol Ann Tomlinson, 2005

One of the unfortunate things about adulthood is our propensity to think kids don't know how to read us. But they <u>do</u>. They can also tell when we're being genuine, and when we're being inauthentic or condescending. Most importantly, they know a powerful teacher when they see one. Students know a powerful teacher when they hear one. And, they know a powerful teacher when they *learn* from one.

This Chapter—*What Do Kids Know?*—explores student attitudes and perceptions, and includes feedback from students coming from a multiplicity of backgrounds, races, ethnicities and cultures from many states. These students' names have been substituted with pseudonyms as have the names of their teachers. Each is "real-world," however, and each has a real story to tell, under more-than-not usual circumstances. Student perspectives about their teachers are, at times, remarkably telling—and in the context

of powering-up teaching, are profoundly insightful.

Students' perspectives about their teachers should not be discounted when we look at our efforts to power-up teaching in all classrooms. Young people can discern high expectations—and typically respond healthily to teaching that conveys a belief in their abilities. Although a student's perspective on his or her teachers can be funny, tragic, and even puzzling—it is rarely anything less than truthful.

"She Teaches in a Mattered Way"

In a middle school in southern California, my team and I were on a typical "walk-through" to get a feel for what was happening in the building; a simple visit in which we were directly engaging both students and teachers in dialogue as we made our rounds. Upon entering a seventh grade Science classroom—you know—a grade level and subject area combination that can be most challenging, we began to witness an extraordinary blend of academic rigor, authentic student engagement, and deep learning. As the lesson was ongoing, I squatted down beside Derrick, one of those students, and—whispering so as not to disturb the lesson or his peers—asked him some probing questions. Derrick responded with answers about the lesson's objectives and the teacher's qualities, but then he made a comment that truly struck me: he said, "*She teaches in a mattered way."* Looking up at the teacher, I could see she had her students captivated with a chemical process. I whispered to the Derrick, "What does that mean, she teaches in a mattered way?" and he responded:

"Dr. Wise, she teaches in a mattered way. Everything she does matters-- and we only do things that matter."

After leaving the classroom, I relayed to my colleagues what this student had said, and asked them what they themselves had observed. The teacher's principal smiled. "That student is spot on—she [the teacher] *does* teach in a mattered way. I just never thought of it in those terms before."

Neither had I. But the student's take on his teacher's effectiveness, I felt, evidenced a certain wisdom that should not be discounted. And what he was describing is what we strive to see in every classroom. What struck me as terrific was a student's uncanny ability to describe his teacher's work so aptly.

Subsequently, while engaged in research centered on more causal teaching behaviors that effectively facilitate *On-Task Learning*, I continue to recall this student's insightful comment. It simply resonated. By ensuring that each minute of classroom time added value to the learning process, his teacher was as powerful and impactful as any I had ever seen in the practice. Better stated, she

was doing what we all seek to do: teach *"in a mattered way."*

"If Mr. Wise would organize his vocabulary words strategically, he'd find that his students would learn their meaning more deeply, and would actually retain their meaning."

While serving in my fourth year as a high school music teacher, I began attending graduate school at night to pursue a Master's in Educational Leadership. At the beginning of that year I was determined to make my teaching rigorous, and as a start I insisted that my Band, Orchestra, and Music Theory students memorize a 100-term music vocabulary list. After all, if they were going to be lifelong lovers of music—or possibly professional musicians or music teachers themselves—I was certain they needed to know terms like *vivace, allegro con brio, con legno,* and *senza sordino*. Further, I was convinced that their memorization of the root, origin, and definition of such terms might be useful in their Language Arts classrooms. (Like a lot of relatively new teachers back then, I just wasn't yet thinking strategically about reading or writing across the curriculum.) I pressed the students to memorize their music terms, pressed parents to help them practice memorizing, and imposed classroom use of some of the terms daily. 100 terms. What was so hard about something so seemingly simple?

Ironically, one of those students was the daughter of Dr. Nancy McGhee, my graduate school professor. While attending Dr. McGhee's Master's-level class in the teaching of Advanced Language Arts one evening, I heard her skillfully announce, *"If Mr. Wise would organize his vocabulary words—strategically—he'd find that his students would learn their meaning more deeply, and would actually retain their meaning."* Somewhat embarrassed, I listened as Dr. McGhee used my less-than-masterful vocabulary mandate as an example of *non-strategic* instruction. I listened as she restructured the assignment to strategically organize my class's vocabulary words into concept categories: volume, speed, style, etc. Dr. McGhee had already—with her daughter—rearranged *my* vocabulary words, *my* music terms so that she and her daughter could master them together. Her daughter ultimately excelled on the assignment.

I was fortunate (and humbled) to learn from Dr. McGhee and from her daughter Megan a very straightforward fundamental: The strategic sorting of instructional information makes that information easier to understand. Placing information in context allows the information to resonate with relevance—and consequently renders it far more germane to life than rote memorization possibly could.

That simple (and admittedly humbling) experience led, in part, to the research and development of behavioral Indicators that became a part of *Power of Teaching* that include *advanced sorting of materials,* providing for *Relevant Academic Practice* and application with *Real-World Relevance.*

"Acting White"

"Come on . . .At the end of the day, Joey, somebody's got to pick up the trash."

Roland Fryer's profound piece, *Acting White (*Education Next, *Winter 2006)* is a thought provoking article that analyzed research on peer-to-peer popularity among students of different races and ethnicity (African-American, white, Hispanic). The research correlates perceived popularity of individual students to their grade point average. According to Fryer, the popularity of white kids tends to rise as their grade point averages climb. But not so for non-whites. In his article, Fryer pointed out that popularity does *not* rise for Black kids as their GPAs climb; on the contrary, their popularity among same-race peers dramatically declines as their academic performance improves. The correlation between climbing academic growth and declining popularity was even more severe for Hispanic kids.

The study was both shocking and disturbing. At the time I read Fryer's work, I was serving as the school superintendent in Jacksonville, Florida trying to get my school board, our

3

community, and my fellow educators there to adopt the most rigorous high school graduation standards in the State of Florida. There was much discussion on how increased demands might hurt our rates of student success (including their grade point averages); it was also feared that by imposing greater rigor, we would increase an already abysmal dropout rate. Painful conversations were frequent: Is it reasonable to think *all* kids could qualify for college? If not, who decides which ones aren't going to take courses that could qualify them for higher education? Do we as school leaders unilaterally make the call? Or do we have a duty to prepare *all* kids to have choices upon high school graduation? The discussions were intense and often heated. I went from community meeting to community meeting pitching my proposal. It appeared surprisingly divisive, and the school board discretely asked me to delay a "formal" recommendation (that is, a public recommendation for their actual vote on the issue) for another month so that we could all further "work the community." The delay appeared warranted, and it occurred.

During that one-month period we delayed the school board vote, I attended yet another business leaders' forum pitching higher academic standards for *all* our kids—not just those some *thought* were college-bound. One well known lawyer—an individual I had respected—chastised me publicly, stating:

"Come on...At the end of the day, Joey, somebody's got to pick up the trash."

Frankly, I was uncharacteristically speechless, and profoundly saddened. This was the very community I had grown up in; the one I had returned to, hoping to make a difference. The room remained silent for many seconds, and those seconds seemed like hours to me. I realized the audience was waiting for a response. I finally blurted out:

"Maybe you're right. But it won't be our *kids.* Our *kids are going to college."*

Lame, perhaps. But at its core, it's what I believed then. And continue to believe. Not much more was said at that gathering. I was proud when the new—and far more rigorous—standards were approved by the school board on a 7-0 vote the following month.

Notably, during that one-month period preceding the board's vote, I used the Fryer article in one of my quarterly book studies with students from each of our 28 urban middle schools and 19 urban high schools. Typically, about 60 students came to these discussions, and I'd asked them to read the article and prepare to discuss it. And discuss it we did:

One middle school boy:

"Dr. Wise couldn't you find something with more recent data

to support the premise [Fryer's article referenced data from the 1990's release of his work]."

I was taken aback by the precociousness of this adolescent. At his age, I had never even looked at the date of supporting material in an article. I remember thinking: *Are we in for a lively discussion or what?*

One high school girl:

"I see this at my school. I am a good student. I have to hide my books in the neighborhood. I get put down if they see me with [books]."

I tried not to reveal my frustration as she went into more detail. In the back of my mind a thought played over and over: *We have a lot of work to do. A lot.*

Another student:

"We [students] can do something about all this prejudging stuff. It's not like we all have to fit in tight boxes."

At that, I remember thinking *"Well maybe there's hope."*

The discussion with the students went on for some time, and was profound in many ways. I remember feeling terribly proud of these students as I listened to them. At the time I was to close the session, I impulsively decided to share with them what the business leader had said earlier in the month—the line about "…at the end of the day, Joey, *somebody* has to pick up the trash." When I related what I had finally said in response I asked "What would you have told him? One middle school student immediately responded, loudly enough for all to hear easily:

"Dr. Wise, that why you [adults] need to turn this diversity stuff over to us; we'll be inventing some THING to pick up the trash."

Brilliant.

"I Believe She's Rushing."

One of my favorite elementary schools in Wilmington Delaware always provided me with meaningful instructional walk-through opportunities—and I loved being there. One morning I arrived late for a scheduled visit, and had hurriedly asked the principal to select three classrooms that would demonstrate teaching practices that she would gauge as: (i) high level, (ii) medium level, and (iii) low level. This type of request had always given me great insight into a principal's craft as instructional leader— and it tends to ensure I get to see real samples of the schools capacity, not just a showboat-type example. The principal responded "Sure. But I really want you see all that I've planned, especially Ms. Orb's Kindergarten class—they are working on vowels and she is proud of

5

the lesson she prepared. She wants us to see it."

We had to hurry to get to the other classrooms the principal had planned for us to visit. A good bit late, we arrived at Ms. Orb's classroom, where the kindergartners were on their reading rug, huddled around Ms. Orb. Because of our timing, she was trying to pace the lesson so we could see the essence. Unfortunately, it was nearing their lunch period.

I sat quietly with the group on one of those tiny chairs designed for 5 year olds, and Ms. Orb tore hastily into the planned activity. The little guy I was seated next to gazed at me briefly, then leaned towards me, as if he wanted to whisper something confidentially to me. Tilting my head towards him, I waited, and he said ever so astutely *"I believe she's rushing."* At that point it took all of my inner strength to not lose it.

The truth was, the teacher *was* rushing. This little guy knew it. And he probably knew it was my fault, since I'd been expected earlier. We can *never* underestimate the perceptual abilities of our kids—even our youngest—when it comes to our teaching. What struck me most was the student's desire to explain that what I was seeing wasn't as good as Ms. Orb could be. He *knew* it. And he wanted me to know it.

"What is the best thing about your school?"
"What is the worst thing about your school?"

On the west side of Chicago several months back, I toured a K-8 school with one of my colleagues. We visited (unannounced) a seventh grade Mathematics classroom. I saw immediately a young man wearing a smart, bright looking t-shirt from my alma mater, Florida State University. Imagine that, way up in Chicago! Because I was there for purposes other than *Power of Teaching* observations, I had no qualms about directly engaging students. Crouching down beside him, I whispered "Where are you planning on going to college?

"I'm going to FSU."

[I was delighted, and continued]:

"Why FSU?"

"Football."

"So, do you play football?"

"No."

"Okay . . . What do you want to study when you get to FSU?"

"I don't know. What do they teach?"

The good news was that *someone* had piqued his interest in college. The bad

6

news was that whoever had piqued this child's interest had not provided critical follow-through information that he—and so many kids—need. This is especially true for kids who would be first-in-their-family to attend college.

The seventh grade Mathematics class continued. Unfortunately, and almost unbearably, instruction was being delivered in such a crude, thoughtless, and cavalier manner that even I was becoming indifferent to it all.

I then asked my young acquaintance how long he had been at the school. He'd attended there since Kindergarten. I learned from the young man that his attendance was good, that he had never committed a behavioral infraction, and that he was well-liked.

"What is the best thing about this school?"

[He paused before answering.]

"I guess it's that I know everyone . . . I like that."

"What is the worst thing about this school?" I asked.

Usually this question is one that students demonstrate discomfort or delay answering. Without hesitating, however, this well-mannered seventh grader gave me his candid reply:

"The teachers."

"Really? What makes you say that?"

"They don't care. They don't know their stuff."

I was stung by his candor. Rising and stepping to the rear of the room, I simply paused and listened as his teacher droned on. She appeared oblivious to her students' uniform disinterest. There was no misbehavior. But there was no engagement. Just day-dreaming students and a teacher who didn't seem to care.

Immoral?
Tragic?

Or simply the status quo in schools where low expectations for kids abound?

As you will find, use of *Power of Teaching* has to start with prepared teachers who want to do the right things—and to do things right. All others need to be counseled into other professions—those that are away from our classrooms.

"Mr. Wise, if you read this far, please check this box."

One of my favorite teaching memories dates back several years, where I thought all 260 of my high school music students would benefit from a "critical listening" project over the course of a 9-weeks grading period. I mean, what wasn't brilliant about assigning students to listen to great music by some of the great masters of the Baroque, Classical, Romantic, and Contemporary Periods—especially if those students were teenagers?

Going into the assigned project I relied on what I thought was my good rapport with, and the high levels of motivation among, my students. The assignment—I was sure—would expose them to college-like work; it would give them a lengthy period of time (all 9 weeks) would require cooperative work, and they would be listening to recordings on high-quality stereo equipment outside of regular school hours.

Reasonable? That assignment equated to 2600+ listening sessions over the 9-week period. Unknown to me at the time, students were criticizing my logic, but I subsequently learned that they were careful not to criticize the intent (at least out-loud.) I stood by my premise—lots of group work, after school hours would be good for them and they would each have to make adequate progress over the course of the 9-weeks—and get started right away. (I was supremely confident at the time. After all, I had just been named *Teacher of the Year* at the school—*certainly* I knew what I was doing.)

On the last few days of the grading period I was flooded with most of the 2600+ separate assignment sheets turned in. I could not possibly read all of these and make good on returning them to my students with timely feedback. I asked a couple of other teachers to help bail me out, and we held a private evening party to read the student assignments (or to at least make the students think they were all being read by me.) As we did our own cramming one of my colleagues read out loud something embedded into one of her answers:

"Mr. Wise, if you read this far, please check this box."

My colleagues chuckled. This student knew that I had been unrealistic in structuring the assignment. And perhaps a little too proud to admit it as things had progressed. And there I was, desperately getting help from other teachers to "cover" the fact that I lacked the ability to individually read all that I had assigned.

Ultimately, I came clean with all of those students that year. What shook me was their response: They were amused, but clearly not surprised. To this day—more than 20 years later—I occasionally encounter one or more of them in my work. Some are professional musicians, while others have gone on to other fields. Ironically, each cannot resist reminding me of that flawed assignment so early in their lives. By the way, each received a letter grade of *A* if his or her 10 "critical listening" sheets were submitted on time. All in all, however, I think we were in agreement: the assignment was a bust in terms of academic growth.

At this point of my teaching career, what should I have known to be able to better handle this situation? What teaching behavior should I have tapped to power-up my own teaching? What would *you* have done? Did my motives appear honorable to you? I hope so, because they were sincere. But, were they well conceived . . . ?

"It's a Frickin' Elephant!"

And even if you still don't believe that kids are deeply discerning, you must know about the "frickin' elephant." Phonics-based reading in progress.

Educator, John Plunkett in Winter Park, Florida recently shared with some of his colleagues about an obviously discerning elementary school student, during classroom reading time, who pointed at a picture in a book about zoos and said, *"Look at this! It's a frickin' elephant!"*

The teacher: "What did you call it?"

Student: *"It's a frickin' elephant! It says so under the picture."*

And so it did... caption under the picture → "African Elephant"

"With all Due Respect..."

When accompanying a group of elected and business officials to tour a KIPP school in Newark, NJ, I encountered an astonishing interaction with a seventh grade student while visiting her math classroom.

We arrived at the school and were greeted by a gregarious principal who reminded his faculty and students via public address system that they had visitors: *"We welcome Dr. Wise, superintendent of schools from Jacksonville, FL and some members of his community. ...Students, please remember to show them great respect and be courteous."*

After a few classroom visits, and picking up on some of this KIPP school's rituals and routines, I repeatedly heard two key phrases: 1) *"I respectfully disagree"* and 2) *"With all due respect..."* The more I heard these phrases, the more intrigued by the work of this school with its wonderfully engaged faculty and students.

You probably know that KIPP schools (<u>K</u>nowledge is <u>P</u>ower <u>P</u>rogram) are public charter schools that serve predominantly students from minority backgrounds and from poverty, often deep poverty. Aspiring to and preparing for college is a mantra among KIPP educators for each of their students.

In one seventh grade classroom, I sidled next to a young girl deeply engaged in her work and the work of their teacher. After a few *"I respectfully disagree"* preambles required by the teacher when students were in-fact asked to disagree with one another on how to solve certain math problems, I asked my young acquaintance some of my favorite questions. The last few questions are captured as part of the dialogue documented below:

"Are you going to go to college?"

"Yes Sir."

"Great. Where do you think you will attend?"

"I am going to Brown University in Providence Rhode Island."

[Playing to my own unfortunate stereotyping of a student from a poverty background] *"Brown, wow. Do you have a backup?"*

"Maybe Cal, Berkeley."

[Borne out of my still persistent stereotyping] *"Well, do you have a second backup if that doesn't work out?* [assuming someone had told her about easier admission schools such as a community college.]

"What is your name again?'

"I am Dr. Wise, visiting your school from Florida."

"With all due respect Dr. Wise, I am only in seventh grade. I don't need a backup plan. All I need to do is set my goals high and work hard to get there."

The student was wonderfully respectful to me, and she was wonderfully candid. I had preached so much to colleagues about the dangers of stereotypes in the work of education. Never again would I consciously allow stereotyping to skew my thinking about any child. With all due respect we should all reap the benefit from my experience with this young lady from Newark, NJ. She will go far!

When we teach in ways that lack meaning, lack effectiveness, or lack in authenticity, kids know. It is incumbent upon us to ensure that classroom experiences of all our kids are led by teachers who care, teachers who are authentic, and teachers who teach with high levels of effectiveness. ***Power of Teaching*** is dedicated to helping instructional leaders help those teachers who care and who approach their work with great authenticity by applying science to the art—to their artistry of teaching.

Chapter Two provides the purpose of ***Power of Teaching***—*the Science of the Art* and layout of this book for use by instructional leaders and teachers.

Chapter Two
The Purpose

The most under-utilized resource in public
education is the classroom teacher.

--Maribeth Smith,
  CTAC Senior Associate
  for National School
  Reform

Power of Teaching has a two-fold purpose: First, to systematically organize 44 key- established- and highly-effective teaching practices and behaviors that we have known about for a long time. Second, and perhaps more pragmatic and important, the work behind **Power of Teaching** was intended to identify powerful and more *causal* teaching practice behaviors only recently understood through research in neuroscience—and through quantifiable examination of the way human beings actually sort, learn and filter information. *Causal* teaching practice refers to educator behaviors that more likely *cause*—rather than simply correlate to—student learning and academic growth.

Michael Walls, former urban superintendent, trusted friend and advisor reminded me of Ron Edmunds powerful influence on the work we do. When advising me on **Power of Teaching** Dr. Walls said, "Remember Ron Edmunds, Joey. *'We can, whenever we choose, successfully teach all children whose schooling is important to us. Whether...we do it must finally depend on how we feel about the fact that we haven't done it so far.'* " (Edmunds, 1979). I didn't remember this Edmunds comment, but I do now. Dr. Walls went on to reflect on his discussions with Larry Lezotte, who clarified that Edmunds did not actually say *all children can learn*, but Edmunds research documents the evidence and power behind the notion that *all* children can learn.

Focusing on the way teachers *facilitate* learning instead of focusing solely on the content of what is taught, **Power of Teaching** provides a concentrated and measured tool to help power-up teachers' work every week, every day, every hour, and every minute they're engaged with students. The core objective is to demonstrate that the *how* of teaching is as critical as the *what* that is being taught. Historically underestimated, the way we communicate with our students is vital; "chalk & talk" just doesn't cut it anymore. Truth is, it probably never did.

If we are to reach students meaningfully, we have to acknowledge that our work involves more than simply mirroring what we grew up with. We must recognize and accept a multiplicity of learning styles, along with a willingness to flex to those styles without giving up rigor. And that's a tough balance.

"We can, whenever we choose, successfully teach all children whose schooling is important to us. Whether...we do it must finally depend on how we feel about the fact that we haven't done it so far."

--*Ron* Edmunds, 1979

Ultimately, if we are to reach *all* kids in a meaningful way, we have to consider practices that affect not just retention of information, but the way in which a child learns to think and processes cognitively. We have to accept that children, regardless of their economic, cultural, racial or ethnic backgrounds, do not learn in predictable ways, or at defined intervals.

In America, like in other well-developed nations, we continue to witness sluggish academic progress with our students in too many schools and classrooms, despite lofty language, an economic edge and high aspirations. To break free of an illogical structure—that has become markedly comfortable for far too many—the nation as a whole has to rethink the *how* of classrooms that work. Pat Deck, a highly regarded teaching expert, and one who lent masterfully to two school districts where I served as superintendent of schools, asserts that this must be done in a way that helps teachers tap into their fundamental beliefs about their work and "what it means to be a teacher." This may in-fact be the only way that teachers can begin to feel truly empowered to *teach,* and not simply comply with often artificial

standards. To *teach* effectively requires empowerment of our teachers—and an investment in our students beyond what has been permitted to date. Again, Pat Deck provided profound advice to me for instructional leaders: *"...changing beliefs and behaviors [about teaching] is hard work. It does not happen... through evaluations..."*

The *Reformers* and The *Defenders of the Status quo*

Randi Weingarten, who was appointed president of the American Federation of Teachers in 2008, has spoken about the longstanding camps in education. Weingarten asserted that "one must declare membership in one of those two camps and then, to remain a member in good standing, reject every idea that comes out of the other camp." As Weingarten asserted her leadership more forcefully at the start of 2009 she describes her disdain for the divide between the so called "reformers" and the so called "defenders of the status quo" as exhausting, and counterproductive" (Weingarten, 2009). Both of these groups of campers and frankly all associated with educating our youth have ideas that should be considered and eventually qualified; however in the trading of ideas, most all ideologues have missed important components necessary for improving the experiences and outcomes for students, often in defense of surviving within and protecting their education camp.

12

Several months after AFT President Weingarten was named to her important role, Arne Duncan was confirmed as the new U.S. Secretary of Education as part of the Obama administration. Just prior to his senate confirmation, Secretary Duncan called for us to "...raise standards dramatically and improve teacher quality." Duncan went on to assert that "We must do dramatically better...and we must stop doing what doesn't work." (Klein, 2009).

We cannot afford to miss any longer, the importance of effectively balancing the *what* with the *how* associated with teaching.

The *WHAT*

Since the 1980s we have largely shifted our education policies to focus on teaching content and *what* standards should be adopted, *what* requirements should be imposed for teacher hiring, *what* accountability standards schools should be held to, *what* assessment data should educators review and report, *what* qualities ensure that teachers are highly qualified (under NCLB) *what* constitutes AYP (Adequate Yearly Progress) for each school, *what* scheduling design is appropriate for high school courses, *what* courses should be offered or mandatory at the high school level . . . A steady drumbeat, the *what* persists as the primary—and often the only—question upon which policymakers focus. No one disputes that the *what* in

education is important. However, so much focus on the *what* and measurement of the *what*—without commensurate focus on the *how* of teaching—results in sustainable academic mediocrity. This extreme and narrow focus on the *what* also perpetuates a persistent pattern of talented teachers and principals leaving the profession regularly in great numbers.

Obsessive commitment to only an isolated component of *any* endeavor results in failure and in preK-12 education, and into "grades" 13 and 14 (college), we have ignored teaching quality for far too long. Like the caged bird that beats itself against the bars of the cage—believing that the bars will eventually give way—we fail to ascertain whether the cage has a door that may already be open. After so much work and extreme focus on the *what,* we must now sufficiently consider the *how* of our work, and the pivotal relationship between the *how* and the *what.* This single-mindedness on the *what,* however well intentioned, has over years left many teachers powerless in their teaching. It continues to drive away from the profession many smart, committed professionals who would otherwise be long-serving, capable educators. The practice as it stands now is often demoralizing, and in many ways destructive. And after all these years, we have little to show for the effort of so much imbalanced focus on the *what.* With a healthy blend of the *what* with holistic focus on the *how* we can provide

13

implementation know-how among teachers to power-up their teaching for *all* their students *all* the time.

Single-minded focus on the *what* in virtually all states, counties, cities and townships has left teachers feeling that education reform is something done *to* them—and not *with* them. The extreme position in which we find ourselves and our profession also finds kids being relegated to a number, a dot on a data wall, and a mere statistic as part of a sub-group or ability group. Now is the time to shift to a healthier balance by focusing on our teachers and all their students as individuals. Raising student achievement through the teachers themselves is of great importance. Assisting teachers so that they can better focus on the more *causal* aspects of driving learning for each individual student may be even more important for instructional leaders.

Clarifying the Work in Instructional Improvement

If we are to shift to a more healthy balance—meaningfully—the way our students receive instruction, focusing on the *how* of teaching is paramount. Simply put: We need to balance the *what* with the *how*.

We also need to include Coaching and Support with the *What* and the *How*. Together all three best provide for each teaching professional to reflect, and continuously improve and add power to his teaching.

Clarifying the Work in Instructional Improvement

What Standards
What Curriculum
What Assessments
What Instructional Material
What Strategies
What Training

How we Plan
How we Question
How we Engage
How we Pace
How we Communicate
How we Teach

WHAT

Planning

HOW

Teacher Reflection

Coaching Techniques
Coaching Protocols
Coaching Processes
Coaching Relationships

COACHING

Copyright © 2010 *Atlantic Research Partners*

Hopefully, this Venn diagram helps to illustrate the power which is lacking in so many of our current generation classrooms, especially those classrooms without a full complement of kids who'd *get it* anyway and sometimes do well overall even with a weak or ineffectual teacher.

Power of Teaching calls for combining and balancing of the following:

- Improved classrooms processes (data-driven determinations of what works—and doesn't work—in classroom interactions)
- Increased productivity (modifying what we used to identify as classroom *work*)
- Increased *meaningful* engagement
- Enhanced awareness of learners' neurological and cognitive capacity
- Identification of actual (measured) *time-on-task* between teachers and students.

15

Commonly, in classrooms with a high ratio of learners from disadvantaged or disabling circumstances—and/or in classrooms with a teacher who has not achieved mastery of his teaching craft—we have disproportionate and inadequate academic growth. We must work with almost surgical-type precision to support educators and their students in those venues if sustainable differences are to occur. In effect we must create *power* in the craft of all classroom teachers—teacher, by teacher, by teacher—and *with* those very teachers. We have to focus not on *correlations* to student academic gains, but on the *causal* behaviors of our educators that result in those gains.

Power of Teaching was designed as a developmental instrument and continuous feedback system to support teachers in enriching their teaching. Its purpose is to enable participating teachers to shift their instructional behaviors to achieve one core goal: to minimize the ineffective and maximize the effective.

Master Teachers

A man who works with his hands is a laborer; a man who works with his hands and his brain is a craftsman; but a man who works with his hands and his brain and his heart is an artist.
　　　　-- Louis Nizer

Master teachers are truly artists. It may seem unnecessary to focus *Power of Teaching* on our master teachers—after all, they've reached a point of fine practice, terrific fluency, and truly potent lesson planning and delivery abilities. Master teachers' classrooms often evidence exceptional dynamics, and they find successes in unexpected and novel ways. So why focus on them?

Rarely do venues for teacher development dive deeply into teacher behavioral performance and strategies to also power-up the work and influence of master teachers. Master teachers are often the best suited to mentor, teach and coach less-experienced or thinly-talented individuals. Although master teachers currently have multiple avenues to assist others (e.g. professional learning communities, lead teacher assignments, asymmetrical teacher chat rooms—you name it), these venues are not enough. Largely, many teacher development venues continue to focus on the *what* and rarely on the *how* of influencing learning through teaching.

The research behind *Power of Teaching* can also empower master teachers so they can better support their less-proficient teacher-colleagues in seeking to improve ways in which they reach their own students. Master teachers can help probe for more *causal* factors in teacher-student interactions, and can dramatically assist other teachers in the honing of communication skills—skills so crucial in affecting student willingness and readiness to learn.

16

In typical teacher development venues, educators are left to complete assignments that:

- Generally have them look at assessment data (the *what*);
- Requires them to attend to a schedule (again the *what*); and
- Frequently contemplate which students should be taught certain courses or pulled out for remedial work (yet again, a *what* of teaching).

Imagine when master teachers can take time to observe a less-than-fluent teacher's classroom work, and offer specifics on how that teacher can power-up the work and its effectiveness. Imagine how a master teacher can build upon his or her own repertoire through observation and training—and ultimately continue refining his/her already strong practice.

Frankly, it's time for us to balance the *what* (and measuring the *what*) with the *how*—and measuring the *how* —in teaching, even with our master teachers.

In Dr. Michael Gazzaniga's exciting book *Human* (2008), he describes shopping at Nordstrom to bring home a point about perception:

If you go shopping at Nordstrom and enjoy the piano playing while you are shopping, you are in a positive mood. When you see a red purse you like, you are more likely to buy it because of this positive mood. However before we enter the store, I might tell you, "Don't let the piano playing go to your head. They do that to put you in a good mood so you'll buy more." Then when you see that purse, you will be more conscious about deciding whether you like it.

Just as Dr. Gazzaniga has raised awareness of what many would have considered background music, so too should we bring effective (more causal) practices to the top of mind for our master teachers. This will improve their artistry and will help them more deeply contemplate their practice with greater "fluency". Raising such awareness will also further empower our master teachers to develop every so masterfully their more novice teacher colleagues.

Master Teachers and Conscious Competence

While working with a group of educators from the Philadelphia and Baltimore public schools in Philadelphia, it occurred to me that master teachers must be consciously aware of their high degree of competence in order to also help develop more novice teachers.

The four stages of competence described by Howell (1982) provide a suitable framework for where we need to orient our master teachers

Unconscious Incompetence - this is the stage where you are not even aware that you do not have a particular competence. You don't know what you don't know.

Conscious Incompetence - this is when you know that you want to learn how to do something but you are incompetent at doing it.

Conscious Competence - this is when you can perform a particular task or skill and you are conscious about every step in performing the process.

Unconscious Competence - this is when you finally master it and you do not even think about performing the skill such as when one learns to ride a bicycle successfully (Howell, 1982). Superintendent Lloyd Martin refers to this level as automaticity.

Most of our master teachers are so fluent and adept in their teaching strategies, they operate at the unconscious competence level or stage. Re-orienting master teachers to the conscious competence level or stage through *Power of Teaching* observations and behavioral data collection in their own classrooms cannot only help them reorient to the conscious competence level but also help them improve their own areas of opportunity for increased effectiveness ratios.

Whether you see this work of continuous and accelerated improvement in our preK-12 and even grades 13 and 14 (college) work as the most important social justice and civil rights work of our times or you see this work as the most important economic development work of our time, hope-   fully to see its dire importance.

Six Power Sources in Teaching

Domain 1: **Focusing and Engaging Minds**

Power Source 1.0 . . . . *Cognitive Connections for Learning (& Teaching)*
Power Source 2.0 . . . . *Pacing & Productivity for Learning*
Power Source 3.0 . . . . *Transitions, Processes & Endings for Learning*

Domain 2: **Managing Learners for Learning**

Power Source 4.0 . . . . *On-Task Learning*
Power Source 5.0 . . . . *Differentiated Teaching to Accelerate Learning*
Power Source 6.0 . . . . *Aligned Expectations to Macro-Organization*

Chapters Dedicated to the Six Power Sources

Components of the Power Sources have been debated, researched and in various ways codified in recent years. Others have been evident in what we often think of as the literature of best-practices in the preK-12 profession and into grades 13 and 14 (college). These valuable components have always lacked, however, a cohesive quality required for the *how* of teaching to be easily developed in each school. *Power of Teaching* is designed to bridge the gaps, and establish a cohesiveness that hopefully makes a difference for teachers and school leaders. From 1935 to 2009, much has been written on the practice of teaching. *Power of Teaching* is a means of joining together strong practices that work.

In Chapter Three, the approach to *Power of Teaching* is presented.

In Chapter Four the design, organization and uses of *Power of Teaching* data collection instrument are outlined and addressed.

In Chapter Five, Power Source 1.0—*Cognitive Connections for Learning (and Teaching)* is explored. Oddly, only in recent years have educators begins to develop an intense focus on neuroscience, and analyzed how teacher-awareness of its complexities can power-up cognitive connections for kids in every classroom, every learning day.

Power Source 2.0—*Pacing and Productivity for Learning* in Chapter Six acknowledges that— for many years—scholars have known that effective *pacing* of instruction leads invariably to improved use of time (productivity) in a classroom. For too long we have failed to identify, clarify, and develop this source of teaching power to improve learning and academic outcomes from our work.

Power Source 3.0—*Transitions, Processes & Endings for Learning* in Chapter Seven addresses a surprising reality: Even effective teachers lose substantial contact time with students over the course of an academic year due to "down time" at the beginning and ending of lessons, and frequently during transitions within a given lesson. Measuring this component of the work—and being aware of its significance on a day-to-day basis—can make a crucial difference in *how* a student learns.

Chapter Eight provides a separate and distinct Power Source 4.0—*On-Task Learning*. This component of the work is identified separately from other Power Sources for a reason. Although one might argue that *On-Task Learning* Indicators could very easily be duplicative of *Pacing and Productivity for Learning* Indicators within *Power of Teaching*—the argument would be weak. *On-Task Learning* involves not just pacing or productivity; it also involves focus and substantive pre-lesson planning.

Chapter Nine tackles the important dynamics of Power Source 5.0—*Differentiated Teaching to Accelerate Learning.* Multiple scholars have contributed substantially to effective Indicators of this teaching domain, but none have done so more potently than Carol Ann Tomlinson and Cindy Strickland. Their work has been crucial, and groundbreaking. The Indicators for flexible grouping and *Differentiated Teaching to Accelerate Learning* can be used to powerfully improve both teaching and learning. While differentiation is receiving much time and attention, the work is translating into support to classrooms that has resulted in almost a too-little-too-late scenario, especially as we work to better include students with disabilities and multiple proficiency levels into our regular classrooms. More inclusion is the right direction, and it is the law. Support to teachers in differentiating their work for multiple ability levels must increase. Power Source 5.0—*Differentiated Teaching to Accelerate Learning* and Chapter nine are largely focused on these needs.

Chapter Ten, and Power Source 6.0—*Aligning Classroom to the Macro-Organization* is about the commanding effects of alignment: Alignment of purpose, alignment of practice, and alignment of materials and tools. Whether one serves in a "centralized" school system (where all work is aligned from top of the organization downward) or in a decentralized system of schools, the significance of aligning purpose,

practice and materials and tools cannot be overstated.

Chapter Eleven— *Systematizing the* **Power of Teaching**—is an analysis of how **Power of Teaching** protocols can be and are used creatively in teacher-to-teacher, and teacher-to-teacher/instructional leader partnerships, 1 on 1, and in small groups.

Why should we invest so much more significantly in teachers and in their teaching craft? I suggest to you that no one could articulate the modern day importance better than economic journalist David Leonhardt.

There really is no mystery about why education would be the lifeblood of economic growth. On the most basic level, education helps people figure out how to make objects and accomplish tasks more efficiently…Education may not be as tangible as green jobs. But it helps a society leverage every other investment it makes, be in medicine, transportation or alternative energy. Education—educating more people and educating them better—appears to be the best single bet that a society can make.

--David Leonhardt, 2009

Whether we see this work of continuous and accelerated improvement in our

20

preK-12 and even grades 13 and 14 (college) work as the most important social justice and civil rights work of our times or we see this work as the most important economic development work of our time, hopefully we can all see its dire importance.

Notes:

Notes:

Notes:

Chapter Three
The Approach

We must help teachers develop their mastery of causal behaviors.

--Pat Deck

Colleague Bill Slotnik, Founder and Executive Director of CTAC—the *Community Training and Assistance Center,* and I have had multiple and sometimes fiery discussions on educational issues. We always find agreement on two fundamentals. First, school reform is not simply a plan to solve a finite set of problems, it is something far deeper, and requires continuous refinement. Second, true reform, when it occurs, cannot be sustained when implementation is done *to* teachers rather than *with* and *for* teachers.

The second point may sound simplistic and perhaps trite. It is neither. In truth, heavy-handed mandates demonstrably undermine what should be our core—and mutual—mission: improving lives. Viewing teachers as adversaries (as some parents, school leaders and commentators do) overlooks a simple truth: Teachers—more than classroom environs, more than visual enhancements, and more than the Internet—have the greatest impact on how our children learn, and what they learn. Think back to your own childhood, and the adults who inhabited your world growing up. Then, think about the ones who altered that world. In most cases, it was a teacher whose teaching made the difference.

When we focus on teaching—on what is effective teaching and what is not—the bottom line is this: Teaching *behaviors* influence student learning to an astonishing extent. To maximize a teacher's impact on student learning, our work has to be contemplated in ways that will actually support the work teachers do.

Since certain teaching strategies, techniques and behaviors have been found over time to be more effective than others, some states and certain higher education institutions began codifying those practices that have been found to be most effective for teaching and more causal to learning. Specific behavioral approaches to more rigorously develop the practice of teachers were among the more progressive. Two approaches happen to be Florida-based. Charles and Clifford Madsen at Florida State University developed one of the earliest treatments through *Teaching/Discipline* (newest ed., 1998). The State of Florida Department of Education developed FPMS—the *Florida Performance Measurement System* (1989). Although separate initiatives, both formed rigorous and behavior-based developmental opportunities through which teachers could improve their effectiveness.

Power of Teaching leverages these behavioral approaches farther and is premised on a key notion: We must help teachers convert their less-effective teaching behaviors and practices into higher-level practices if we're going to make a difference. For teachers to *cause* increases in student achievement, teachers must have clear interactions with students that work, and decrease those classroom interactions we know to be ineffective or less-effective.

In developing instructional clarity, we must ensure we are doing our work in an atmosphere of respect and collaboration to help teachers to effectively power-up their teaching.

When discussing some of the research behind **Power of Teaching** with Bill Slotnik, we delved into a deeper discussion on the requirements of educational leaders to also provide professional working conditions that lead to teachers being psychologically-safe and open to changes in their practice. Bill went on to reflect that the approach to **Power of Teaching** appeared different than other methods which address the *how* in teaching in oft isolated and artificially disconnected ways. The approach of **Power of Teaching** is indeed meant to add science—that is behavioral science—to the art of teaching. Bill put it quite nicely after reviewing an early manuscript of **Power of Teaching**: "There is a science to the art of teaching."

Power of Teaching uses data collection instruments to document effective and ineffective teaching behaviors (see Chapter Four). The data collected is gathered to gain an understanding of what is and what is not working for an individual teacher, and to offer supports when patterns of ineffective behaviors are observed. It is crucial to remember that the behavioral data collected is not designed—nor should it ever be used—as an arsenal to undermine an individual teacher's work. **Power of Teaching** has as a main purpose to *assist* in objectively analyzing what works. Helping teachers to measure their ineffective teaching or less-effective teaching behavior is as important as measuring effective teacher behavior—primarily to gain a deeper understanding of how the classroom teacher can become a more *causal* influence on advancing student achievement—it must never be punitive!

At its crux, **Power of Teaching** is about measurement, development, and support: Measurement of behaviors, development of practices, and support of teachers. **Power of Teaching** is designed to improve the ratio of effective teacher behaviors to ineffective teacher behaviors.

Power of Teaching is comprised of 2 Domains and 6 Power Sources for powering-up a teacher's practice.

Focusing and Engaging Minds
(Domain 1)
1. *Cognitive Connections for Learning (and Teaching)*
2. *Pacing & Productivity for Learning*
3. *Transitions, Processes & Endings for Learning*

Managing Learners for Learning
(Domain 2)
4. *On-Task Learning*
5. *Differentiated Teaching to Accelerate Learning*
6. *Aligned Expectations to Macro-Organization*

The two Domains and six Power Sources provide a method to leverage highly-regarded research to use as a measure to discern effective (more causal) teaching vs. unproductive (and therefore ineffective) teaching.

One might ask why do this now, and in this way—particularly after so many well-regarded researchers have over time published volumes on the subjects of teaching and teacher efficacy. *Power of Teaching* establishes one complete system, pulling together the substantial amount of highly valuable literature on our profession, assembled as a "toolkit" for the work we do. This toolkit is a resource for educators at all grade levels, and applicable to all subjects in preK-14.

Power of Teaching is both behavioral and granular in nature. If we are going to greatly improve instruction in grades preK-12 and through grades 13 and 14 (college) to better meet the needs of all students in our communities, we must examine our teaching practices and behaviors and how we support teachers in their teaching. To change behaviors, leaders must understand them—and their impact upon students. Meaningful change involves not only transformation of skill sets and knowledge; it requires adjustment of attitudes, and a keener understanding of what affects kids—cognitively, socially, and emotionally. And it sometimes requires a shift in what we value.

We can change attitudes about teaching by objectively examining the work we do. We can change and improve skills and knowledge among our teachers and instructional leaders and we should, but neither is sufficient in isolation.

We can also make great strides at shifting our values and recommitting to our once closely held values. If you don't believe me, re-read any one of Jonathan Kozol's books. They continue to break one's heart.

When you change teaching behavior for improved results, you have to tap into the cognitive, the social, and the emotional—which, when standing alone, are insufficient to achieve and sustain the changes we need.

Power of Teaching is not an evaluation tool. It is not a tool to be used for firing teachers, and it is not, in and of itself, a school improvement plan. *Power of Teaching* is applicable across all curriculum and subject areas—and it

25

does not address test preparation, or discreet academic subjects.

Power of Teaching is a developmental resource for achieving highly effective teaching; consequently, it is crucial that constructive recommendations accompany discussion of any patterns of inadequacy. By now you have likely discerned that ***Power of Teaching*** is all about powering-up teaching—not driving away teachers.

Before we delve into the real work of ***Power of Teaching***, a few words about w*ith-it-ness*, versatility, and multi-tasking—each truly crucial for our teachers to recognize and employ.

The concept of *with-it-ness* (albeit a made-up word) has been well documented in the literature on teaching pedagogy. Among the most prolific are the works of Jacob Kounin (1983) and Brophy (1996). *With-it-ness* refers to "remaining 'with it' (aware of what is happening in all parts of the classroom at all times) by continuously scanning the classroom, even when working with small groups or individuals."
Ginger Hopkins, an executive with Northwest Evaluation Association (NWEA) characterizes the same trait in a broader concept. Hopkins refers to *versatility*—a teacher's ability to move from student to student, activity to activity, and to/from mode, module, or technique in ways that best facilitate student behavior and drive achievement. Modern day terms for *with-it-ness* and

versatility include but are not limited to *multi-tasking*.

With-it-ness, versatility, and multi-tasking characterize positive, productive teacher behaviors, but they are not measured as discreet and separate categories of effective behaviors in ***Power of Teaching***. Instead, they are underlying components of much that is measured—and are evident in the effective practices that are established through ***Power of Teaching*** observations.

Chapter Four
Observation Instruments

Teaching is an art . . . but there is a science to it too. What we're doing is using the science to "power up" the art of teaching.

--David Sundstrom

The Observation Instrument illustrated at the end of Chapter Four is a critical component of *Power of Teaching*. A tool for collecting teaching behaviors as those behaviors are observed, it provides observers a means to later analyze with the teacher what is working best, for the teacher, and what is not.

As previously mentioned, the Instrument is divided into two primary domains: Domain 1—*Focusing and Engaging Minds* (Side 1 of the Instrument) and Domain 2—*Managing Learners for Learning* (Side 2 of the Instrument). Each domain contains three Power Sources, and those Power Sources specify behaviors that are numbered and organized to identify particular actions that have been clinically established to either:

1. Enhance teaching and learning,
   or
2. Decrease teaching effectiveness.

Each teaching behavior that *Power of Teaching* research identifies as "effective" is specified on the right, and matched on the left with the teacher behavior that is on the other end of the efficacy spectrum (ineffective). This formatting enables the observer to readily record observed practices without extensive searching throughout the Instrument. By linking effective and ineffective teaching Indicators to each individually numbered domain, the Instrument empowers observers to focus less on format layout and more on the behaviors being observed.

Observers should note that certain behaviors occasionally appear in more than one domain i.e., use of *general praise* may be found in Power Source 1.0 and in Power Source 4.0. This is because these teaching behaviors power-up a teacher's teaching in more than one sphere of influence.

To summarize the organization of the Instruments, there are two Domains and six Power Sources:

27

Domain 1: **Focusing and Engaging Minds**
Power Source 1.0 . . . . *Cognitive Connections for Learning (& Teaching)*
Power Source 2.0 . . . . *Pacing & Productivity for Learning*
Power Source 3.0 . . . . *Transitions, Processes & Endings for Learning*
Domain 2: Managing Learners for Learning
Power Source 4.0 . . . . *On-Task Learning*
Power Source 5.0 . . . . *Differentiated Teaching to Accelerate Learning*
Power Source 6.0 . . . . *Aligned Expectations to Macro-Organization*

Organization and numbering of the Power Sources links corresponding effective and ineffective teaching Indicators within the same field. The organization and numbering are simply designed to enable the observer to find, with ease, specific categories of behaviors being observed.

Guiding principles for the use of the *Power of Teaching* data collection instrument

1. A minimum of 25 uninterrupted minutes observing teaching behavior to ensure full coverage of the sources of power being observed.
2. Other than during embedded assessments, do not use periods of testing or other student assessment activities as a time to collect *Power of Teaching* data. (Testing and assessment sessions are important components of

teaching and learning, but are not appropriate activities for *Power of Teaching* observations— except under those limited circumstances when teachers are using test data as part of Power Source 6.0—*Aligning Classroom with the Macro-Organization* in Indicator 6.3—*Strategic Use of Relevant Student Performance Data.*)

3. Teaching behavior should be coded (tallied) in "real time" as it is observed. No coding should take place outside of the actual period in which a behavior is witnessed.
4. Code only what is seen or heard (not what is intended or concluded).
5. Make vertical tally marks in bundled of fives—on the right-side for effective (more *causal*) teaching behaviors and on the left-side for unhelpful or ineffective behaviors.

28

6. Do not interact with the teacher or students during *Power of Teaching* data collection. Visit classrooms regularly to minimize your presence impacting interactions and instruction.

7. Collect data during the observation; don't evaluate.

Calculating Efficacy Ratios—How and Why

A classroom observation should occur only within Domain 1—**Focusing and Engaging Minds** or within Domain 2—**Managing Learners for Learning**—one domain at a time, and no more than three power sources at one time. Certain developmental activities for teachers might call for observations in fewer than three power sources.

Notice that, on the observation instrument, cells are available for making tally marks for each instance a behavior is observed. Cells are available for the observer to total his tally marks within a single power source. This allows for the comparison of the number of tally marks on the ineffective (left) side of the power source area with the number of tally marks on the effective (right) side of the power source area.

Calculate the mathematical ratio of:

The total number of *effective teaching behaviors* observed
to:
The total number of *ineffective teaching behaviors* observed

A ratio calculation allows the observer to report back to the teacher his or her effectiveness ratio in a given power source, which then enables the teacher to compare that observation to his/her personal best from prior observations.

The total number of tally marks within a single Indicator can also be used when a certain teacher and the applicable instructional leader(s) have as a goal for the teacher to improve an effectiveness ratio in one behavioral area. Note however, that the Indicators are grouped so that all contribute to the overall behavioral analysis within a single power source. It is best to focus holistically on a power source to maximize the positive effects that can be derived from *Power of Teaching*.

Notes:

29

Notes:

Atlantic Research Partners   *Power of Teaching*   Focusing & Engaging Minds

SOURCE	INEFFECTIVE	Tally	Sum	Sum	Tally	EFFECTIVE
1.0 Cognitive Connections for Learning (& Teaching)	1.1 Negative Reinforcing Verbals/Nonverbals					1.1 Effective Verbals/Nonverbals
	1.2 Ineffective Grammar/Diction					1.2 Effective Grammar/Diction
	1.3 Questioning with Insufficient Wait Time					1.3 Questioning/Sufficient wait time
	1.4 Harsh/No Redirection to Incorrect Responses					1.4 Effectively Guided Incorrect Answers
	1.5 Indifferent Engagement of Students					1.5 Application with Real-World Relevance
	1.6 Use of General Praise					1.6 Applied Specific Academic Praise
	1.0 Total/Ratio	%			%	**1.0 Ratio/Total**
2.0 Pacing & Productivity for Learning	2.1 Missed Opportunity to Adjust Pacing When Needed					2.1 Use of Differentiated Pacing
	2.2 Introduced New Concept/Activity or No Comprehension Check					2.2 Checked for Academic Understanding
	2.3 Extended Discourse					2.3 Specific Dialogue to Excite Learning
	2.4 Unproductive Remediation or *Busy Work*					2.4 Applied Grade Level Rigor
	2.5 Indifferent Engagement of Students					2.5 Engagement w/ Real-World Rigor
	2.6 Use of Standalone Discourse					2.6 Effectively Applied Academic Rule w/Examples
	2.0 Total/Ratio	%			%	**2.0 Ratio/Total**
3.0 Transitions, Processes & Endings for Learning	3.1 Ineffective/Unclear Transitions					3.1 Made Lesson Transitions Explicit/Clear
	3.2 Irrelevant Opening Activity					3.2 Opened the Lesson/Topic with Clarity
	3.3 Downtime/Wasted Minutes					3.3 *Bell-to-Bell* Instruction
	3.4 Moved to New Concept w/No Practice					3.4 Provided for Relevant Academic Practice
	3.5 Allowed/Created Fragmentation or Unproductive Discourse					3.5 Maintained Academic Flow/Pacing
	3.6 Irrelevant/Overuse of Recall Questioning					3.6a Differentiated/Strategic Use of Questioning
						3.6b Strategic Use of Higher Order Questioning — 3.6b1 Required Student Analysis of Topic
						3.6b2 Required Student Academic Reasoning on Topic
						3.6b3 Required Student Synthesis on Topic
						3.6b4 Required Student Academic Judgment of Topic
	3.0 Total/Ratio	%			%	**3.0 Ratio/Total**

Atlantic Research Partners   *Power of Teaching*   Managing Learners for Learning

Power of Teaching, second edition. Copyright © 2010 by Atlantic Research Partners, LLC. Reproduced by permission of Atlantic Research Partners, LLC.

Teacher_____ Date_____ Time_____ **Subj/Grade.**_____

SOURCE	INEFFECTIVE	Tally	Sum	Sum	Tally	Sum	Sum	Tally	EFFECTIVE
4.0 On-Task Learning	4.1 Circulated with no Explicit Purpose-or Remained at Desk								4.1 Circulated & Assisted w/Instructional Purpose
	4.2 Group Chastisement/Consequences								4.2 Redirection/Disciplined in Private
	4.3 Academic Concepts without Examples/Non-examples (Standalone Discourse)								4.3 Made Student-centered Meaning w/ Examples or Non-Examples
	4.4 Counting/Sorting Materials on the Fly								4.4 Advanced Sorting of Materials
	4.5 Use of General Praise								4.5 Applied Specific Academic Praise
	4.6 Delays Behavior Management								4.6 Stopped Misconduct Strategically
	4.0 Total/Ratio	%			%				**4.0 Ratio/ Total**
5.0 Differentiated Teaching to Accelerate Learning	5.1 Missed Opportunity for Activity Grouping or Grouping with no Strategic Intent Apparent								5.1a Flexible/Groups for Accelerating Learning — 5.1 Flexible Grouping for Accelerating Learning
									5.1b Strategic use of Heterogeneous Grouping
									5.1c Strategic use of Homogenous Grouping
	5.2 Under-utilized Classroom Furniture								5.2 Strategic Use of Furniture to Flexibly Group
	5.3 Under-utilized adult(s) to enable learning								5.3 Strategic Use of Adult(s) to Flexibly Group
	5.4 Under-utilized achievement/Activity Data								5.4 Strategic Use of Data to Flexibly Group
	5.5 Ignored Student Engagement/Responses								5.5 Accentuated Academic Responses with Linking Words
	5.6 Missed Opportunity for Emphasis or Amplifying								5.6 Emphasized Salient Academic Points
	5.0 Total/Ratio	%			%				**5.0 Ratio/Total**
6.0 Aligned Expectations to Macro-Organization	6.1 Unrelated *Busy-work Materials* in Use								6.1 Approved *Materials in Full Use*
	6.2 Non/Misused/Under-Resourced Walls								6.2 Teacher Arranged Artifacts In-Use
	6.3 Non/Ineffective-Use of Student Performance Data								6.3 Strategic Use of Relevant Student Performance Data
	6.4 No Student Work Posted								6.4 Teacher Arranged/Displayed Student Work
	6.5 Non/Misuse of Word-Walls								6.5 Grade-level Endorsed use of Word-Walls
	6.6								6.6
	6.7								6.7
	6.8								6.8
	6.0 Total/Ratio	%			%				**6.0 Ratio/Total**

Teacher_____ Date_____ Time_____ **Subj/Grade**_____

Domain 1

Focusing & Engaging Minds

Notes:

Chapter Five
Cognitive Connections for Learning (and Teaching)

Exceptional advances in human brain research in recent years have led to a reframing of the issues teachers confront. What we now know about the brain and the way it functions is staggering: as a typical individual maneuvers through childhood, tens of billions of neurons are interconnecting through tens of trillions of synapses—often seamlessly. The way our minds develop—and process information coming at us from all senses—is far more complex than previously imagined, and full understanding of the brain's power remains far from complete. What we have learned, however, affects the *how* of effective teaching in a substantial way.

Leveraging the complex processes by which kids learn and assimilate concepts has everything to do with timing and with stimuli provided by teachers. Recognizing the complexities of kids' minds—and responding to their different learning styles—is an enormous means of empowerment and responsibility for teachers. The purpose of Power Source 1.0—*Cognitive Connections for Learning (and Teaching)* and Chapter Five is to focus on ways to maximize cognitive connections, and to optimize the sustainable learning that occurs when those connections are made.

Teacher training programs have increasingly recognized the substantive role of neuroscience in teacher preparation. As new dimensions about brain plasticity are discovered, we have begun moving away from some clearly outdated—and often harmful—teaching practices that frequently resulted in "warehousing" kids and the "monolithic" effects of grouping and managing students for teaching and learning (Christensen, 2008).

We now know that individuals perceive the world through different and innate "wiring" and filter those perceptions through varying biases and prejudices they learn as they mature. We can influence the biases and prejudices through education—but not very well if we assume that all humans process and retain information in the same way. They don't. And after generations of losing students who just didn't get traditional (whole group) *chalk 'n talk* teaching, we've begun to recognize the need to effectively differentiate instruction. (See also Chapter Nine and Power Source 5.0—*Differentiated Teaching to Accelerate Learning.*) Sporadically, and sometimes inelegantly, we've begun trying to reach kids who from younger generations would have been ignored—or put on a track far from that which was university bound.

We have only recently begun to seriously acknowledge that we lose high school student drop-outs long before they stopped coming to school. By late middle school, many whose brains are not "wired" for rote instruction simply begin "checking out"—or alternatively becoming behavioral problems—to avoid the dreary reality of being adjudged *stupid* or incapable of learning. This is not to say that kids don't engage in stupid behavior on occasion—they do, sometimes at astonishing levels. But stupid behavior is not limited to children, and most often has nothing to do with cognitive development.

Kids often *believe* they're "stupid" or incapable of learning when in fact the issue is not intellectual capacity, but anomalies in synapses; in how their brain processes. Cognitive, social, and emotional development appears to occur through neurological processing. "...neurons that fire together in time will wire themselves up. And the more often a set of neurons fire together, the more likely it is that they will fire again together and form an easier and easier representation so it will be easier and easier to get that set of neurons to fire off together and wire up together...It's believed at this point that the firing together of information in time will bind that information together and say, 'okay this is a chunk of information which is occurring on a regular basis statistically in your environment, it must be important - pull that together and make it easier for your brain to respond to it'. And we think that has something to do

with the basic units in which the brain is going to perceive the...building blocks" (Tallal, 2008).

Many know that Microsoft's Steve Ballmer loves to be profound. Well, in April of 2009, in an interview with Businessweek Magazine, he may have made his most profound statement to date: ". . . if we don't acknowledge that my 11-year old- son [is] consuming content differently, we'll go extinct" (Adler, 2009). With the advent of technology-based interventions come many programs, of which I remain a staunch advocate due to certain research-proven characteristics and a review of the student performance data and success rates associated with these interventions and protocols. These include the following:

- Scientific Learning *Fast ForWord*
- Scholastic *Read 180*
- Scientific Learning *Reading Assistant*
- Alternatives Unlimited *Drop Back In Academies*
- University of Nebraska affiliate *Class.com*
- *Achieve 3000*
- Exxon Mobil Foundation affiliate *Reasoning Mind*
- Carnegie Learning *Cognitive Tutor*
- Arizona State University affiliate *Adaptive Curriculum*
- Compass Learning

Even with these and other effective technology-based solutions, especially for struggling or disenchanted students, intervention must remain driven by a teacher. Not driven by content. The need for every teacher to continue to improve his craft will remain a high priority even as computers help teachers manage the work of teaching. Part of this continuous improvement is through increasing the teacher's cognitive connections to his students to the extent possible.

Verbal Cues

Previously, little was known about the relationship between verbal cues and other teacher-led stimuli to student processing of information. Yet the human brain remains highly adaptable well into geriatric ages—and with the right interventions can process information in radically different ways if stimulated sufficiently e.g., stroke victim rehabilitation protocols. When it comes to students who appear to be having difficulty mastering concepts, the determination of whether interventions are necessary—and then which interventions are appropriate—becomes critical.

Power Source 1.0—*Cognitive Connections for Learning (and Teaching)* provides six key Indicators of teaching behaviors. These teacher behaviors, when strategically and carefully applied, can improve the ways our students process information.

1.1 Effective Verbals/Nonverbals

Voice tones, patterns and character of voice greatly influence a student's processing of the actual spoken word. Positive and dynamic auditory stimuli particularly aid those kids who take their "lead" from verbal cues. Negative—and occasionally even neutral—voice tone, patterns, or character can undermine the educator's message, and impede understanding (and the willingness to understand). In Indicator 1.1—*Effective Verbals/Nonverbals,* the observer should record data observed relating to positive and reinforcing teacher voice tones (effective) on the right-side of the *Power of Teaching* instrument and too loud, too soft, grating, or harsh teacher-voice timbre (ineffective) on the left-side of the instrument.

Patterns of Speed in Teacher Speech

A review of the research of Thomas & Leeper, 1978, following Carver, 1973, revealed that students are more likely to comprehend verbal messages at teacher talk speeds from anywhere between 200 words/minutes (Thomas & Leeper) and 150 words/minute (Carver, 1973). Due to radical changes in stimuli brought about by technology and communication venues in recent years, some now argue that children of the millennial generation (children born after 1983) have grown accustomed to "rapid-fire" speech, and may be actually less tolerant of slower teacher speech patterns than children of

37

prior generations. If the observer observes that speed of teacher talk may be affecting the way students are processing an observed lesson—either as an effective teaching behavior or an ineffective behavior—the observation should be coded with a left-side tally in either Indicator 1.1—*Effective Verbals/Nonverbals* or Indicator 2.1—*Use of Differentiated Pacing* depending upon the Power Source being impaired.

Quality of Speech

Quality of speech can be observed for in Indicator 1.1—*Effective Verbals/ Nonverbals.* For more than 60 years, researchers have established a strong causal connection between effective teacher speech patterns and powerful teaching; those teachers found to be exceptionally masterful at teaching were shown to have significantly better speech patterns than mediocre or weak teachers (McCoard, 1944).

McCoard (1944) also found that good teachers use more variety in speech e.g., rate of speed, volume, phrasing, quality and pitch, than less-effective teachers. Diehl & McDonald (1956) found that teacher "nasality and breathiness" interfere with a teacher's ability to effectively communicate with learners. Subsequently, Diehl, White, & Satz (1961) found that classroom lectures with more variation in vocal pitch from the teaching lecturer were rated as very good or good by participating students.

Coats & Smidgens (1966) when studying teacher dynamism found, among undergraduate students, that students remembered much more from "dynamic presentations which were delivered from memory with much more vocal inflection, gesturing, eye contact, and animation." Coats & Smidgens (1966) also found that "static delivery" did not induce increased lecture recall.

Good & Brophy (2003) documented the importance of verbal and nonverbal behavior to promote intensity and enthusiasm for lesson content. "In addition to the words being spoken, everything about a teacher's tone and manner communicates to the student that what is being [taught] is important and that [students] should give it full attention and ask questions about anything they do not understand." In the same work, Good & Brophy also provided what intense and enthusiastic verbal and nonverbal behaviors are not. "…we do not mean pep talks or unnecessary theatrics. …we mean that teachers [effectively convey] their own reasons for viewing a topic as interesting, meaningful, or important and project these reasons to [their students through their teaching.]" (See also Indicator 2.3—*Specific Dialogue to Excite Learning.*)

Positive Voice Timbre Reinforced by Nonverbal Communication

Also part of 1.1—Effective Verbals/ Nonverbal is voice timbre. *Timbre* is defined by the 2006 Random House Unabridged Dictionary as the characteristic quality of a sound, independent of pitch and loudness, from which its source or manner of production can be inferred.

The teacher's voice timbre is of significant importance for effective teaching. Teacher voice and verbal efficacy are compounded by nonverbal teacher behaviors. Effective verbal behavior can be positively amplified by the way the teacher positions herself in relation to the students, and can also be negatively neutralized by physical placement and use of other nonverbal gestures and behaviors. Colleague Tom McDowell, national curriculum and special education expert for whom I have great regard and have learned much, reminded me that teachers remaining "on a perch" without movement about the classroom, and without using varied and effective nonverbal gestures can undermine their otherwise positive elements of their verbal behaviors, without being aware of this effect.

It is important for nonverbal teacher communication to support and sustain positive voice timbre and all uses of the voice. It is also important for teachers to avoid well-documented traps preventing effective use of nonverbal communication. Chaiken, et al., (1974) documented traps that teachers can fall into such as when forgetting to use appropriate eye contact, lacking attentiveness, responsiveness, or providing assistive encouragement such as leaning forward or using confirming head nodding. When using *Power of Teaching* Observation Instruments and observing teachers effectively avoiding these *traps*, code this effective teaching behavior with a right-side tally in Indicator 1.1—*Effective Verbals/Nonverbals*.

When contemplating Indicator1.1— *Effective Verbals/Nonverbals* with colleague Brenda Tanner, I was reminded of the widely endorsed practice of using sharp and intensively focused teacher eye contact with students as a means to influence on-task behavior and clear communications with the student(s). As you will find with *Power of Teaching*, some behaviors are best coded as effective (right-side tally) on one Power Source and ineffective (left-side tally) in another Power Source.

When making cognitive learning connections for kids—in Power Source 1.0—*Cognitive Connections for Learning*—it is important to ensure students are not coached into defensive or shut-down mode when challenged by a teacher's question or facilitation through eye contact that is too intensively administered. Regardless, the conversations about powerful teaching must be ongoing, lively, and engaging among instructional leaders if we are to build the type of classroom observations that are truly helpful and energizing to our teacher colleagues.

Effective Verbals include Clarity, Volume, and Projection

Verbal clarity, volume and projection produce positive and productive auditory stimuli. Teachers who speak in a monotone, speak too softly, or speak at inopportune (non-strategic) times undermine the instructional message they seek to convey—and often lose their students well before the end of a lesson. Typically, these ineffective teaching behaviors are not borne out of incompetence or a lack of kindness— they're simply behavioral patterns readily modifiable through positive coaching. In Indicator 1.1—*Effective Verbals/ Nonverbals,* the strategic use of verbal cues, positive voice tone and appropriate pitch—and the varying use of each, depending on the teacher's intended message—would be effective Indicators of positive teaching (to be coded on the right-side of Indicator 1.1—*Effective Verbals/Nonverbals*).

Vague Speech and Clarity

When a teacher's phrasing is vague, other positive aspects like volume, projection and timbre can be negatively affected. The following are examples of these points:

(Setting: Middle School Classroom; verbatim monologue on Christopher Columbus):

Teacher:

"Realistically, the Queen was insistent that Columbus reach new land for her. I think there was not known, so much, that a continent such as ours, within terrific reach existed. So, Columbus, set forth, actually to please his Queen, but went east, we, he, thought he was going to go east, but actually the boats, his boats did in-fact go west. When he landed, he landed much by surprise in America, well it was the Americas, even though we didn't call it that. It was an island in the Caribbean, and the rest is history."

[Verbatim recorded Duval County Public Schools, FL 2007.].

Clarity, Same Lesson

Teacher:

"Queen Isabella of Spain wanted to expand her empire; Columbus persuaded her that he could help her by establishing a shorter trade route to India than was then known. He claimed that if she provided him three ships, he could travel west from Spain instead of east and reach India faster than all others. He was wrong. At the time, neither he nor anyone in Europe knew that the continent of North America

existed. The Queen provided him three ships, and he set sail in 1492. When he reached the Caribbean islands near the North American continent, he thought he'd reached India. Columbus even named the inhabitants of those islands Indians."

Samples of effective teacher behaviors for right-side coding in Indicator 1.1— Effective Verbals/Nonverbals:

- Voice is rhythmic, peaks and valleys in delivery
- Students should appear engaged
- Voice timbre should be appropriate to the population being taught
- Underlying intent or tone is genuine, caring, focused
- Appropriate energy; crisp, clear enunciation,
- Imagery represented in speech
- Concise sentence structure
- Appropriate use of humor words or humorous style/animation

Samples of ineffective teacher behaviors for left-side coding in Indicator 1.1— *Negative Reinforcing Verbals/Nonverbals:*

- Screeching
- Yelling,
- Shrillness
- Overuse of slang, inappropriate, or informal terminology
- verbal tics that become irritating (ex. "ya' know")
- Sarcasm
- Monotone
- Mumbling
- Other put downs

With data collected for Indicator 1.1— *Effective Verbals/Nonverbals* the observer, when providing feedback to the teacher, will be able to more effectively help develop the teacher's acumen around those verbal and nonverbal interactions which are positive and reinforcing.

41

1.2 Effective Grammar/Diction

Most teacher preparation programs, especially in the English Language Arts, have stressed the associative nature of learning language and languages. Less often these programs stress that this associative process by which language is deeply learned can also yield the learning of poor grammar and language skills and poor diction among our teachers' students.

According to Orville Boyd Jenkins (2006) "Language is not information, but the format for processing information -- not explanation, but mastery. Drill and practice helps to impress the models of the languages into the learner's subconscious. Conscious awareness of the models and structures may help the learner master the structures rather than be limited by them. ...the models must be mastered, in order for thought to flow into communication. This is done through practice and use."

Jenkins went on to apprise us that "language consists in social events, communication events, *interaction* with other people. In common teaching approaches, language is often *isolated from its practical context.* ...languages are used by social groups...to manage their relationships and cultural roles, obligations and interrelationships."

While Jenkins was primarily addressing the teaching and learning of a second or third world language, the premises address the importance of a teacher's use of grammar. While the teacher may be teaching music, mathematics, science, social studies, or something else—her use of grammar in English (or another primary teaching language of the classroom) continues to reinforce, teach, re-teach or un-teach the very effective use of grammar that we expect our students to master for a productive adulthood.

With data collected for Indicator 1.2— *Effective Grammar/Diction* the observer, when providing feedback to the teacher, will be able to more effectively help develop the teacher's acumen around his use of grammar and diction to best help students associate and therefore replicate proper uses of grammar and diction themselves.

Superintendent Lloyd Martin refers to Ruby Payne's construct of formal vs. informal register to help teachers help kids distinguish neighborhood and household talk from classroom or business talk.

Samples of effective teacher behaviors for right-side coding on Indicator 1.2— *Effective Verbals/Nonverbals:*

- Use of appropriate terminology/slang for the culture ("guys")
- Use of student names
- Discreetly expects proper grammar from students
- Discreetly corrects improper grammar of students

- ▪ Articulates a mistake in grammar or spelling made when instructing the class
- ▪ Appropriate grammar including
  - o Verb/tense match
  - o Use of linking words

1.3 Questioning/Sufficient Wait Time

Wait time, or giving a student sufficient time to think about and answer a teacher's question, is one of the most widely understood and agreed upon components of teaching pedagogy. Use of wait time (for thinking and engagement) has been deemed effective for decades. Yet, perhaps because of its age, this powerful tool of fundamental pedagogy appears to be one of the most under-leveraged components of teaching practice today. Like other *Power of Teaching* Indicators, this component of the practice has been established to cause—and not simply correlate to—higher academic achievement. The negative effects of wait time missing from a teacher's practice are significant. Further, Allington (1980) Taylor (1979) Mendoza, Good, & Brophy (1972) and Rubovits & Maehr (1971) all found that effective teachers provide sufficient wait time for students for whom they held low expectations for high achievement.

In the somewhat artificial climate that arises when a teacher is being observed in his classroom, it is certainly understandable for a teacher to generate energy and encourage engaged students to call out the correct answer(s). After all, doesn't that student enthusiasm indicate that the teacher is successfully conveying what he or she is supposed to be teaching? But the energy created by the "calling out" of answers oft times masks underlying deficiencies. Does the teacher call upon those students less-likely to answer a question incorrectly? Does the teacher allow sufficient wait time for an individual student to think through her answer? What would the remainder of the class be otherwise doing if wait time occurred? Might the class become unruly? All of these questions represent legitimate fears of a teacher—any teacher. But in a supportive environment, that fear can be readily overcome.

Wait time can be powerful, especially if other students are conditioned to know that they may be called upon to validate, evaluate, build-upon, or correct an answer provided by their called-upon peer. Generally, wait time creates important self-esteem opportunities for the called-upon student i.e., *"My teacher has high expectations of me and knows I can answer this question correctly."* The experience involves two things: rigor + relationship, and can be the impetus for other *on-task* behavior (from the called-upon student as well as all other students).

Conversely, when wait time is too-lengthy it can be embarrassing and damaging to a child. It can diminish

43

self-esteem and can erode the student's desire to participate or engage. This concern raises another: What is an appropriate course of action when a student who is called-upon really cannot answer the teacher-posed question? The answer is straightforward: re-direct attention by engaging another student, or switch gears to review the concept before engaging the affected student again. Suggested approaches include:

- Ask the called-upon student to call on another student to help her.
- Ask for a volunteer to "help us out on this one."
- Simply switch back to explaining or exploring the concept in greater detail, then follow up by again questioning the affected student.

If uncertain whether the delicate balance of maintaining instructional momentum and classroom dynamics is appropriate, it's always helpful to sound out other teachers for feedback.

Sample effective teacher behaviors for right-side coding in Indicator 1.3— *Questioning with Sufficient Wait Time* include the following:

- Not too much wait time, but not rapid fire questioning – a good balance
- Actual wait time varies, situationally

- During wait time, teacher provides support questions or comments
- Appropriate use of wait time that allows all children to process and provides "think time"
- Sensitive to dynamics of the group
- Have students call upon another student
- Have student repeat correct answer given by previous student
- Give prompts
- Off-line set up for successful responses

Sample ineffective teacher behaviors for left-side coding in Indicator 1.3— *Questioning with Insufficient Wait Time*

- Too long, too short, wait time of fewer than 6 -10 seconds
- Wait time too long and/or creating embarrassing moment for student
- Less wait time for students teacher assumes will not know the answer

With data collected for Indicator 1.3— *Questioning with Sufficient Wait Time* the observer, when providing feedback to the teacher, will be able to more effectively help develop the teacher's acumen around her use of wait time to best help students engage, think deeply, and receive the transfer of knowledge intended for them by their teacher.

1.4 Effectively Guiding Incorrect Answers

Understanding and using successful feedback practices includes taking advantage of the instructional openings an *incorrect* answer provides.

"To successfully engineer understanding, educators have to be able to describe what it looks like, how it manifests itself, and how apparent understanding (or misunderstanding) differs from genuine understanding" (Wiggins & McTighe, 1998). With data collected for Indicator 1.4—*Effectively Guiding Incorrect Answers* the observer, when providing feedback to the teacher, will help the teacher tap into one of the most potentially fruitful classroom resources, that of a student's incorrect answer in the midst of a lesson.

Sample effective teacher behaviors for right-side coding in Indicator 1.4—*Effectively Guiding Incorrect Answers*

- Teacher gives students opportunities to show what they know
- Teacher asks additional guiding question
- Encourages students to explain, comes back to student
- Use as a re-teaching moment
- Requiring respondents to elaborate upon answers to reveal common errors behind the incorrect answer
- Coming back to incorrect responder to ensure understanding of correct response

Sample ineffective teacher behaviors for left-side coding in Indicator 1.4—*Harsh or No Redirection to Incorrect Responses.*

- Teacher does not recognize opportunity/teachable moment
- Teacher simply moves on to next student
- Choral response and not all students respond
- Using only lower order questions without elaboration

With data collected for Indicator 1.4—*Effectively Guiding Incorrect Answers* the observer, when later providing feedback to the teacher, will be able to more effectively reinforce or help develop the teacher's practice in guiding incorrect answers.

1.5 Application with Real-World Relevance

Brian Greene, a professor of physics at Columbia University and author of *The Elegant Universe* and *The Fabric of the Cosmos* wrote in a New York *Times* essay:

...[C]hildren begin life as uninhibited explorers of the unknown. From the time we can walk and talk, we want to know what things are and how they

work—we begin life as little scientists. But most of us quickly lose our intrinsic scientific passion. And it's a profound loss. (Greene, 2008)

In theory, there is consensus on how to most effectively teach scientific and non-scientific principles: use engaging methods requiring analysis, hands-on learning, application, synthesis, and authentic exploration. When learners are required to work and learn using kinesthetic methods, real-world relevance makes the content come alive. When learners are required to compare/contrast Shakespearean works with modern-day Rap or other artists in measured, engaging ways, they have the chance to learn, and retain the principles and knowledge that they are mastering in the moment. *Relevance* does not mean a simple pandering to pop culture phenomena; it simply means bringing a concept alive. Teachers do it by tying each concept to what is tangible to a child. When we love literature or history or philosophy the way so many of us educators do, it can be sometimes hard to go beyond the purity of what we're teaching to *relate* it to students' lives in a way that resonates with them. But love of subject-matter content does not justify indifference to student experience and cognitive needs. To make a concept memorable and lasting to a student, and to preserve a child's innate enthusiasm for being "uninhibited explorers of the unknown" we have to find ways to always make taught concepts tangible and real. We do this by tying it to their real-world experience.

Further importance of teaching with *Real-World Relevance* was studied by Wagner (2008) who provided seven real-world survival skills that "all students must master to get—and keep—a good job in today's global knowledge economy, succeed in college, and be leaders in our communities."

1. Critical thinking and problem solving
2. Collaboration across networks and leading by influence
3. Agility and adaptability
4. Initiative and entrepreneurialism
5. Effective oral and written communication
6. Accessing and analyzing information
7. Curiosity and imagination

Wagner (2008) is perhaps the most compelling of our contemporaries demonstrating that "[if the U.S.] is to remain competitive in the global economy, high school students must master 21st–century skills." Thus ***Power of Teaching*** contemplates Indicator 1.5—*Application with Real-World Relevance* as one key for effective teaching.

Sample effective teacher behaviors for right-side coding in Indicator 1.5—*Application with Real-World Relevance*

- Approach is specific to the population, community

- Directly tied to the task you are working on – not contrived;
- Teacher facilitates real world connections that students bring to the classroom, e.g. using the world series to calculate statistics
- Connecting topic to student, give real world examples, elaborating on subject matter concept within a relevant cultural context

Sample ineffective teacher behaviors for left-side coding in Indicator 1.5— *Indifferent Engagement of Students include the following:*

- Teacher doesn't tie content to meaning for students' lives
- No relevance, irrelevant examples,
- Sole focus in subject matter without relating to common theme/experience in student's world
- Relevance is merely example based and not context-based

1.6 Applied Specific Academic Praise

Brophy (1981) provided a definition for the concept of teacher-delivered praise as a detailed expression of positive teacher response that gives the student(s) information about the value of his or her response. In 1981, Brophy also found that for effectiveness, teacher praise had to be more than a general statement, such as "*nice work*" or "*fantastic*".

Since the 1970s, we have learned that aside from the positive effects of specific praise lay the negative effects of frequently delivered teacher criticism. In more than 12 studies conducted in grades 1-10 classrooms, negative correlations of statistical significance were published on the frequent-use of teacher disapproval and criticism and students engaging in the lesson.

Brophy (1981) reported that teachers praise too infrequently. Anderson (1979) observed that teachers praise about 11% of student (correct) responses. Heines & Hawthorne (1978) Cooper & Baron (1977) and Brophy & Good (1970) all found more frequent praising of students expected to be high performers by their teachers than with students expected to be lower performers.

Power of Teaching advocates that praise must be authentic, specific, and used non-sparingly among students already expected to perform at high levels as well as with students where academic challenges might be perceived to exist. See the positive examples below:

- *"The way you crafted that sentence showed unusual insight into..."*
- *"The way you explained both the concept and its effect demonstrated your understanding of..."*
- *"Your written comparison made me think of a published writer's*

47

work—it was carefully edited content..."

Our review of the research also revealed importance of the following:

- Endorphins activity appears to increase in the brain when a student receives positive feedback--even general feedback.
- Endorphins appear to increase significantly when the positive feedback identifies *with specificity* something the student wrote, said, or did.
- Commensurately, the student associates that intensified "rush" of endorphins with the specific academic work for which he or she received the praise.
- That association—the specific praise tied to an academic activity—strengthens the academic activity to retain greater significance in the student's memory (Lysakowski & Walhberg, 1981).

The implications arising from the use of *Applied Specific Academic Praise* cannot be overstated: specific academic praise powerfully reinforces learning in a highly effective and remarkably memorable way. *Specific A*cademic Praise means going farther than adults— by nature—typically do when commending a student. Instead of saying "Good job!" or "You're *right!"* *W*e simply have to go deeper to be more causal in driving student learning. (See also Chapter Eight and Power Source

4.0—*On-Task Learning*—Indicator 4.5—*Applied Specific Academic Praise*.)

Authenticity in Administering Specific Academic Praise

Certainly a teacher's statement such as *"I really like the way Josiah uses his rich vocabulary in his writing assignment class. The rich vocabulary makes it exciting to read his work"* would warrant a right-side tally mark as an effective teacher practice. Dr. Tanner reminded me that in her practice as a developer of teachers and instructional leaders, that increasingly, she is observing the decreased effect of a teacher starting off her specific praise statements with "I really like..." In the artistry of teaching, this phrase can project inappropriate judgment and lack of objectivity on the part of a teacher. Effective teachers limit their use of statements such as *"I really like the way you..."* They get right to the specific point of the praise with *"The way you..."*

Neuroscience affirms the power of *specific* academic praise along with a *just-in-time* repetition of the academic principle, fact or concept associated with the praise. Deliberate practice of *applying specific academic praise* powers-up two domains contemplated in ***Power of Teaching***: Power Source 1.0—*Cognitive Connections for Learning (& Teaching)* and Power Source 4.0—*On-Task Learning*.

48

As instructional leaders, one of our core duties is to assist teachers in shaping their practice to maximize their effectiveness with kids. Decreasing the use of *general* praise while increasing the use *specific* praise is perhaps one of the most powerful adjustment teachers—veteran as well as new teachers—can make. And it's best accomplished when the teacher consciously targets the particular student response or behavior that was instrumental in earning the praise. This adjustment enables a teacher to create an enduring transfer of knowledge affecting students of multiple ability levels and learning styles.

Because specific praise has long been a part of behavior management, its efficacy sometimes gets overlooked when the focus is on actual teaching and academic growth. Most teachers consciously work to be as positive as possible with students, and to create a positive behavioral climate even on the hardest days in a classroom. Heard in almost every elementary school are things like, "I like the way you're standing in line," "Good job sitting up straight," "Thank you Devin, for raising your hand" and the proverbial and worn-out "Crisscross, apple sauce."

Lysakowski & Walberg (1981) documented some of the most compelling research on the use of praise in education. When appropriately used, praise as a reinforcement of academic connections resulted in learning at the 80th percentile vs. 50th percentile (when praise either was not applied or was applied ineffectively—often as general praise).

Specific praise for behavioral compliance is not specific *academic* praise. Although such praise has merit, it should not be considered as effective nor coded as a right-side tally in Indicator 1.6—*Applied Specific Academic Praise*. Rather, specific praise for student conduct should be considered as helpful (effective or right-side tally) on Indicator 4.6—*Stopped Misconduct Strategically*. That sort of praise might serve Power Source 4.0—*On-Task Learning*, but will not serve Power Source 1.0—*Cognitive Connections for Learning (and Teaching)*.

Examples of General Praise (harmless but ineffective)

- *"Good job Marty"*
- *"Class, I am proud of Cynthia."*
- *"Jeremiah got the correct answer too!"*
- *"I am so pleased with Lauren."*

Examples of Specific Academic Praise (*Powering up the work*)

- "Good job Marty. You used the skip-counting method to add in your head."
- "Class, I am proud of Cynthia. She remembered to conjugate the verb when she drafted her response."
- "Jeremiah got the correct answer too. And, he checked his work by also solving the problem

backwards." [teacher enunciating the word he even more adamantly.]

- "Lauren did a great job. She read her poem, sounding out her consonants very crisply." (Teacher enunciating the word consonants even more profoundly.)

Cognitive Connections for Students from use of Effective (Specific Academic) Teacher Praise

1. Reinforces to students about the value of their competence.
2. Causes students to closely associate their effort with their achievement or problem solving.
3. Causes students to see the type of effort (or thinking) that can yield similar (successful) results (and praise) in the future.
4. Causes students to realize the enjoyment of the specific academic achievement (FPMS, 1989).

A school principal or other instructional coach can assist a teacher in powering up his or her work by helping *measure* the teacher's use of specific praise—specific academic praise designed to provide a greater cognitive punch than general praise. Once he or she has that feedback, the teacher should be purposefully aiming to alter the ratio between specific academic and general praise. By simply adding a few words of specificity to a general statement of praise, a teacher can power-up the effectiveness of the event—and the memory of the lesson.

Remember the elementary student from Chapter One who was obviously discerning during classroom reading time, who pointed at a picture in a book about zoos and said,
"Look at this! It's a frickin' elephant!"

The teacher:
"What did you call it?"

Student:
"It's a frickin' elephant! It says so under the picture."

And so it did... the caption under the picture read
→ "African Elephant"

Should a teacher treat this with teaching behavior commensurate with a right-side tally on Indicator 1.6—*Applied Specific Academic Praise* for the student's accuracy of phonics or with a response that would warrant an observer's right-side tally on Indicator 1.4—*Effectively Guided Incorrect Answer* or both, or neither?

Note that some practitioners discount the use of specific academic praise in early primary grades. In Florida, for example, leaders advocate such in the *Florida Performance Measurement System* for evaluating teacher effectiveness. The premise—for which there appears to be insufficient research—concludes that general praise for students in preK-1 is perfectly acceptable and not to be considered an ineffective practice. Further, specific academic praise is deemed by some educators as not really necessary until about Grade 2.

Power of Teaching requires a more rigorous approach. Specific academic praise must be preferred over general praise for all ages, and for all academic grades. Generic or general praise is not harmful per se. Generic praise ostensibly can have some value. Most importantly, however, generic or general praise—even in early grades—does not create the more causal power to the teaching/learning, transfer, and retention processes at productivity levels created by the effective use of applying specific academic praise.

Notes:

Notes:

51

Notes:

Cognitive Connections for Learning (& Teaching)	Power Source 1.0
From *Power of Teaching* Observation Instrument	

INEFFECTIVE	TALLY	SUM	SUM	TALLY	EFFECTIVE
1.1 NEGATIVE REINFORCING VERBALS/NONVERBALS					1.1 EFFECTIVE VERBALS/NONVERBALS
1.2 INEFFECTIVE GRAMMAR/DICTION					1.2 EFFECTIVE GRAMMAR/DICTION
1.3 QUESTIONING WITH INSUFFICIENT WAIT TIME					1.3 QUESTIONING WTH SUFFICIENT WAIT TIME
1.4 HARSH/NO REDIRECTION TO INCORRECT RESPONSES					1.4 EFFECTIVELY GUIDED INCORRECT ANSWERS
1.5 INDIFFERENT ENGAGEMENT OF STUDENTS					1.5 APPLICATION WITH REAL-REWORLD RELEVANCE
1.6 USE OF GENERAL PRAISE					1.6 APPLIED SPECIFIC ACADEMIC PRAISE
1.0 TOTAL/RATIO	%			%	1.0 RATIO/TOTAL

53

1.1 Effective Verbals/Non-Verbals

Look-fors and Listen-fors

Ineffective	Effective
VERBALS	**VERBALS**
Nasal voice tones	Well-modulated voice tones
Too loud voice tones	Clarity of speech
Too soft voice tones	Well projected voice
Grating voice tones	Varying voice tones
High-pitched voice tones	Melodious voice tones
Harsh voice tones	Crisp consonants
Monotone	Inflection
NON-VERBALS	**NON-VERBALS**
Lack of gesture	Animation
Too loud voice tones	Eye contact with students
Lack of eye contact with students	Gestures

1.2	Effective Grammar/Diction

Look-fors and Listen-fors

Ineffective	Effective
Use of poorly constructed sentences	Use of correct technical vocabulary
Use of 'street' language in classroom	Use of appropriate terminology for the culture
Mispronounced words	Discreetly expects proper grammar from students
Verb/tense mismatch	Discreetly corrects improper grammar
	Verb/tense match
	Correct use of linking words
	Uses students' names

1.3	Questioning with Sufficient Wait Time

Look-fors and Listen-fors

Ineffective	Effective
Random calling out	Strategic use of wait time
Too short wait time	Redirecting questions, when appropriate
Too long wait time	Wait time varies depending on complexity of question
Harsh voice tones	Prompts students strategically
	Melodious voice tones
	Crisp consonants
	Inflection
	Animation
	Eye contact with students
	Gestures

1.4	Effectively Guiding Incorrect Answers

Look-fors and Listen-fors

Ineffective	Effective
Teacher simply moves on to next student	Teacher gives students opportunity to demonstrate what they know
Teacher gives answer him/herself, no check for understanding	Teacher asks guiding questions, scaffolding students
Choral response and not all student respond	Encouraging student, come back to student
	Requires students to elaborate upon answers to reveal common errors behind the incorrect answer
	Uses response as an opportunity to re-teach

1.5	Application with Real-World Relevance

Look-fors and Listen-fors

Ineffective	Effective
Teacher misses opportunity to tie content to students' lives	Associations to students' world are directly tied to what's being taught and is not contrived
Irrelevant examples	Connects topic to students' real-world using examples within a relevant cultural context
Misses opportunities to relate subject matter to common experiences in student's lives	Approach is specific to the population or community
Grating voice tones	

1.6	Applied Specific Academic Praise

Look-fors and Listen-fors

Ineffective	Effective
'Good job!' 'Class, I am so pleased with Katie' 'Well done!' 'Nice work, Shaqueta' 'I am so proud of Gracie'	'Good job Daniel, you used the skip-counting method to add in your head.' 'Thresa, you should be proud of yourself. You remembered to conjugate the verb when you drafted your response.' 'Wow! Vijay you read that passage very clearly, enunciating all the consonants so crisply!'

Notes:

Chapter Six
Pacing and Productivity for Learning

Academic rigor is not faster and louder.
      --Lynn Fardell

When analyzing the practices of the previous 6 years of winning- and finalist-school districts of the highly regarded Broad Prize in Urban Education (see: www.broadfoundation.org) common themes appeared in the practices of these higher performing school districts. These themes in practice include well-aligned curriculum to state academic standards and high-stakes state assessments, systemic and systematic professional development, robust progress monitoring, and strategic use of pacing. Even in rigorous inspections of schools for performance recognition, improvement and professional development, little of our work addresses pacing within a lesson. Power Source 2.0—*Pacing and Productivity for Learning* contemplates those teaching behaviors required for highly effective academic pacing and classroom productivity. Power Source 6.0—*Aligned Expectations to Macro-Organization* (see Chapter 10) contemplates additional alignment

requirements for highly effective practice.

2.1   Use of Differentiated Pacing

Christensen (2008) views the current-day, monolithic learning environments as a backslide from the days of the one room schoolhouse—an era in which teaching practice relied on near-customized student activities geared at the level of skill and readiness of each individual student. Even though Christensen champions greater reliance on Internet and other technologies to achieve greater differentiation among learners, the reality is this: Massive investment in technology for public preK-12 schools will not be sustainable, nor sufficient.

Valerie Levenberg, a former Curriculum and Instructional Chief with Edison Learning once stressed to me:

"I'd rather a child learn math from a computer than from a teacher who doesn't understand math."

While technology will become more and more a tool in public education, it will take much time to reach the maximum potential that technology can offer each modern-day classroom. We have to better differentiate instruction for each and every child every day with or without more access to advanced technology. And a key component of differentiated instruction is the *differentiated pacing* of that instruction.

Perhaps the most compelling case for improvements in teacher-led pacing is the intensity with which we must more effectively include students of varied disabilities, ability, and proficiency into regular classroom activities. Inclusion is the right thing to do and it's the law. Increased and improved uses of *Differentiated Pacing* provides effective teachers strengthened opportunity to individualize instruction within a large class setting.

Sample effective teacher behaviors for right-side coding in Indicator 2.1—*Use of Differentiated Pacing*

- Teacher breaks students out into groups and provides appropriate activities as needed
- Students doing different things; flexible grouping with appropriate activities; observed extended learning opportunities for advanced / quick students
- Teacher recognizes when students are "getting it" and can move on
- Teacher acknowledging students who need additional time and accommodates
- Teacher changes instruction based on results of checking for understanding
- Modifications being made for individual students as needed

e.g., special education, English Language Learners, etc.

Sample ineffective teacher behaviors for left-side coding in Indicator 2.1—*Missed Opportunity to Adjust Pacing When Needed*

- Students are waiting or students have completed their work and teacher doesn't change pace
- Disengaged students
- Continuing to do an activity that should have ended because the concept was mastered
- Frustrated acting students who want to finish and don't have enough time
- Teacher ignoring student requests for change in speed of instruction

2.2 Checking for Academic Understanding

Teacher-posed questions are a means of assessing whether students are grasping lesson content. Checking for understanding along the way—when effective—is discreet, part of "the fabric" of every lesson, and used by teachers to assess their own efficacy-in-progress. It is especially helpful for making mid-course correction in the way information is being conveyed. Indicator 3.6—*Differentiated/Strategic Use of Questioning* is based upon fundamental ways effective teachers check for academic understanding—and it remains a powerful practice.

Stallings & Kaskovitz (1974) contemplated that in handling incorrect student responses, when checking for academic understanding, powerful practice results when the teacher assists the student in creating a correct answer by asking simple questions to the student in err. Simply providing the student the correct answer and then moving to another topic, question, or to another student to seek the correct response does not, in and of itself, relate positively to student achievement gains (Anderson, et al., 1979 & Stallings & Kaskovitz, 1979).

Madeline Hunter (1984) regarded "checking for understanding" mostly in the context of effective teacher behavior as a precursor to understanding the knowledge, concept or skill that was about to be employed in a guided student practice. Equally important and also coded as an effective teaching behavior is teacher behavior probing whether a student acquired the new knowledge, concept, or skill, even without guided practice.

Sample effective teacher behaviors for right-side coding in Indicator 2.2— *Checked for Academic Understanding*

- Teacher uses response cards, thumbs up/down with appropriate follow-up

- Teacher circulates and monitors student work
- An environment is created where it is safe for students to say *"I need help"* or *"I don't understand"*
- Teacher asks probing questions
- Multiple types of checking happening, many opportunities for checking understanding
- Teacher demonstrates they understand why they are checking and how they will follow-up
- Teacher has identified stumbling blocks to learning

Sample ineffective teacher behaviors for left-side coding in Indicator 2.2— *Introduced New Concept/Activity with No Comprehension Check*

- Teacher does not check if students understand
- Teacher moves on too quickly
- Teacher is giving the students information, not probing students' background knowledge
- Questions are less about understanding and more "I gotcha"
- Teacher more focused on time than understanding, sometimes blindly adhering to program
- Teacher moving on without reference to what has been learned or not establishing connections to previously learned topics
- Teacher exhibits frustration and no plans for future re-teaching

63

2.3 Specific Dialogue to Excite Learning

As discussed in Chapter Five, voice timbre, volume and projection make a critical difference in making cognitive connections—see also Indicator 1.1—*Effective Verbals/Nonverbals*. But, speech qualities alone do not create excitement for learning. The *content* of speech, and the way it is presented, obviously have matching importance. Keith (1974) attacked overuse of the "blackboard" and Hiller (1971) attacked vagueness as an impediment to student achievement. Solomon (1964) and Thompson (1960) each provided compelling evidence of the power behind teacher-student dialogue. Wright and Nuthall (1970) provided complementary documentation of their research on the value of one-question-at-a-time teacher practices.

Projecting enthusiasm provides a significant factor in efficacy around Indicator 2.3—*Specific Dialogue to Excite Learning*. There is not-so-new but encouraging news here for instructional leaders: Kids, like adults, respond favorably to enthusiastic presentation of information. Bettencourt (1979) contended that "students react favorably" to teachers who project enthusiasm, and also that projecting enthusiasm can be a learned teacher trait.

Enthusiasm is tied to student perceptions of teacher professionalism, trustworthiness, and overall confidence in the teacher (Gunderson & Hopper, 1977). Notably, Mastin (1963) provided that teacher enthusiasm has a direct and positive effect on student learning when accompanied by other factors (e.g. specific dialogue). Coats & Smidchens (1966) measured college students' ability to remember, and found greater retention of information from "dynamic presentations delivered from memory with much vocal inflection, gesturing, eye contact, and animation." The Coats & Smidchens research is equally applicable to Indicator 1.1—*Effective Verbals/Nonverbals* concerning effective voice, volume, and projection.

Historically, those of us who support teachers in their teaching craft by and large have failed our teachers—by not coaching, mentoring or focusing on dynamism in the delivery of lessons. Bettencourt (1979) through his study of fourth, fifth, and sixth grade school students demonstrated higher levels of engagement as well as *on-task* behavior under the influence of teachers demonstrating enthusiasm in their teaching behavior. Mastin (1963) found that teacher enthusiasm created positive effect among seventh graders in student learning and student attitudes about learning. A follow-on study (Bettencourt, Gillett, Gall, & Hull, 1983) demonstrated yet again the positive effects of enthusiasm as a driver of engagement and *on-task* student behavior during taught lessons.

Aspects of effective teacher enthusiasm documented by Bettencourt (1979) include:

1. Varied, dramatic body movements
2. Animated acceptance of students' ideas and feelings
3. Frequent demonstrative gestures
4. Varied emotive facial expressions
5. Varied words and frequent use of adjectives
6. Active, and wide-opened eyes
7. Uplifting and varied vocal delivery
8. Demonstrated overall-exuberant energy level

Analysis of the work of Nelson, Martella, and Galand (1998), Soar and Soar (1979), and Brophy & Evertson (1976) provided the basis for the following behavioral contributors for effective use of *Specific Dialogue to Excite Learning:*

- Continuity of presentation or academic conversation
- Planned emphasis of key words, key concepts
- Explain, in a convincing way, *why* the content matters
- Focus solely on concepts that matter
- Refrain from vagaries
- Apply lesson structure to learners' level of ability; in communication strategy, apply appropriate "stretching" of each student's paradigm.
- Applies strategically intended repetition that also minimizes overuse (therefore unproductive use) of remediation
- Refrain from overuse or non-strategic use of whiteboard or electronic projection devices without a change in stimuli

Jodi Mastronardi, who leads human capital management strategy for Edison Learning mentioned in a group discussion on *Power of Teaching* protocols about Indicator 2.3—*Specific Dialogue to Excite Learning*. "When a teacher links her knowledge and confidence with a subject matter to her passion for the topic, she can't help but generate excitement for her students. Her enthusiasm is infectious, and students are captivated, looking forward to the next activity – they become engaged with the material without hesitation."

Behavioral impediments to effective use of *Specific Dialogue to Excite Learning* should be coded when observed as left-side tallies in Indicator 2.3—*Extended Discourse or No Enthusiasm:*

- Teacher exhibits behavior is overly gushy
- Teacher exhibits behavior demonstrating bitterness
- Teacher exhibits behavior and treatment of student as an enemy
- Teacher exhibits behavior as extreme overreaction to student behavior
- Can include missed opportunity to excite learning
- Teacher talking at students, without engaging them

- Lecture (talk and chalk)
- Monologues
- Discussion with only a few students

2.4   Grade Level Rigor

Content of a lesson needs to be rigorous for the grade level at which it is presented. *Busy Work* is not evidence of rigor. *Busy Work* is also regarded as ineffective in Indicator 2.4—*Unproductive Remediation or Busy Work*. Along with unproductive remediation, busywork devastates a teacher's ability to provide grade-level rigor. **Power of Teaching** advocates for the position that either of these two ineffective protocols can also impair other sources of power for intensifying a teacher's efficacy.

Lockwood (1978) and others provided evidence of the unhelpful effects of busywork. Over the decades that followed, we have failed to sufficiently train, coach, and develop novice and even seasoned teachers on the critical importance of *rigor*. We speak of academic rigor—but by and large we do not yet go far enough to coach teachers on how to achieve and consistently apply it. In part, because we don't restrain ourselves or teachers from engaging in unproductive remediation and *busy work*.

Other important advice from colleague Brenda Tanner was a note she wrote to me contemplating Indicator 2.4—*Applied Grade Level Rigor*:

"Joey, what about work that is not busywork, but is just not rigorous enough? For example—standards/concepts that are too easy/simple."

Dr. Tanner made a significant point in her note to me. Teachers who miss opportunities to engage kids in optimal and well-planned rigorous work should be observed as ineffective in either this Indicator 2.4—*Unproductive Remediation or Busy Work* or in Indicators listed in Power Source 5.0—*Differentiated Teaching for Accelerating Learning*. (See also Chapter Nine.)

Another common trap for educators in deciding upon treatment of students who have moved ahead of their classmates as well as those who are behind and need re-teaching, reinforcement, or remediation is the teacher's use of technology-driven instruction. Uses of technology-driven instruction can and should be included in **Power of Teaching** protocols. As a fundamental, technology-driven instructional materials to add rigor or to remediate some students while others receive Grade level Rigor from the teacher must be content-centered and not game-centered. Additionally, these resources must be aligned to what the school and classroom professionals are actually held accountable for. Tom McDowell also reminded me that high stakes exams are content-centered or processed-centered and not game-centered. Participating in games and gaming can be instructive but are not the ends when used, they are simply a means (and only when used strategically).

Sample <u>effective</u> teacher behaviors for right-side coding in Indicator 2.4—*Applied Grade Level Rigor* include the following:

- Collaborative learning on complex concepts
- Fully engaged students
- Work is on grade level (or above); appropriate level of challenge for students;
- Work is scaffolded when necessary;
- Work is challenging, purposeful to the students
- Works meets kids in their learning zone
- Appropriate content, vocabulary, language usage
- Effective use of computer remediation

Sample <u>ineffective</u> teacher behaviors for left-side coding in Indicator 2.4—*Unproductive Remediation or Busy Work* includes the following:

- Busywork; too much guided practice that becomes busy work
- Drill and kill
- Work that is too easy (or too hard)

- Not regrouping as needed (e.g. kids staying in remediation group though no longer needed)
- Inappropriate or overuse of computer-based remediation

2.5 Engaging Students with Real-World Rigor

Engagement with *Real-World Rigor*—or what Willard Daggett refers to as "rigor/relevance"—is of huge importance to establishing context in what we are teaching students. It also reaps more productive levels of student engagement, or what Phil Schlecty frequently refers to as "authentic engagement."

The negative complement to Indicator 2.5—*Engagement with Real-World Rigor* is 2.5—*Indifferent Engagement of Students*. Indicators of student engagement include the following:

- Student behaviors demonstrate their access to Real-World Rigor
- Doing assigned individual work
- Verbally participating in the class activities
- Demonstrating active listening to the teacher or other presenter(s)
- Participating in other appropriate lesson-related activities

As a positive example, protocols utilized in the State of Florida's new-teacher observation system (FPMS) stress looking for a teacher estimating student engagement quickly and "not spend[ing] more than 20 seconds visually scanning the classroom to count non-engaged students." This is consistent with behaviorally-based protocols developed by others, e.g. Gallup, Gregorc, etc., where snapshot glimpses are considered valid and reliable behavioral measures.

Effective teachers "give teenagers plenty of chances to be active in the classroom, allowing them to make choices and decisions, without giving up their authority as the teacher, setting up this environment plays to teens' desires for independence and competency. These teachers also...convey relevance and get the students interested even if the subject seems unrelated" to the students' daily lives (Pianta & Allen, 2006).

Pianta found in a similar study of kindergarten through fifth-grade teachers that "Good teachers also interact with their students in ways that show them that their teachers know them and care about them."

Rigor-Relevance-Engagement

Rigor, Relevance, and Engagement fit together like hand-in-glove for effective teachers facilitating effective lessons. Even though *Power of Teaching* observers are asked to code *Applied Grade Level Rigor* in Indicator 2.4 and *Engagement with Real- World Rigor* in Indicator 2.5, overlap may be observed in the classroom of a highly-effective teacher.

In conducting a presentation for educators on the west side of Chicago, one school leader asked how she should think of the difference between Rigor-Relevance and Engagement. After reminding the group of school leaders how important it was for them to know the grade level expectations and pacing schedules for their schools, I shared that there is a difference that will reveal itself in classroom observations between *Grade Level Rigor* and *Real-World Relevance*. The example I gave was as follows:

Real-World Rigor might be asking a math class to calculate recent Major League Baseball statistics for a math class warm-up. *Grade Level Rigor* would be when the same math teacher has directed her class to calculate downturns in the stock market during a defined period of economic study occurring in these same students' social studies classroom. One provides real world examples to work from. The latter addresses both the real world nature as well as the grade-level expectations with a real-world example.

With data collected for Indicator 2.5—*Engagement with Real-World Rigor* the observer, when providing feedback to the teacher, will assist the teacher to further develop his engagement, academic deepening, and behavior management pursuits through rigor and relevance that real world examples and context can provide for his students.

Sample effective teacher behaviors for right-side coding in Indicator 2.5— *Engagement with Real-World Rigor* includes the following:

- Teacher checks that student understands the relevance, purpose, audience, application of what is being learned
- Students are evidencing a connection between their world and the work i.e., using economic example to drive work
- Work is authentic
- Involves problem solving
- Is outside of the textbook
- Students are engaged in learning
- Students are working in textbooks

Sample ineffective teacher behaviors for left-side coding in Indicator 2.2— *Indifferent Engagement of Students* includes the following:

- Students are indifferent to the work that they are doing
- Students are doing work out of compliance rather than engagement
- Students are engaged but there's no rigor or relevance evident

2.6 Effectively Applying Academic Rule(s) with Examples

For students to be able to effectively apply academic rules, after a teaching and learning activity has concluded is a matter of retention. Those who know me well, professionally, also know that one of the reasons I am so high on the neuroscientists and educators at Scientific Learning, is that they introduced and attacked the problem of insufficient memory on the parts of people young and old through their Fast ForWord™ and Posit Science ™ products, protocols and services.

There's a lot of buzz about current day students—also known as the millennial generation: *they are multi-taskers, they are wired differently, they can't go slowly;* all of which we are hearing may be true. Some biologists posit that the brains of humans, and that means the brains of our students, do not compute answers to problems. Hawkins (2004) posits that the brain retrieves answers from memory. "The entire cortex is a memory system. It isn't a computer at all" (Gazzaniga, 2008). Gazzaniga, considering the work of Hawkins, provides us with the following:

1. The neocortex stores sequences of patterns

2. The neocortex recalls patterns automatically—it can recall a complete pattern when given only a partial pattern. When you see only a rooftop over the hill, you automatically know to

expect a building once you cross the hill. A computer would not.

3. The neocortex stores patterns in invariant form. This part of the brain can handle variations in a pattern automatically. When you see your child from the left afar you can recognize him the same as seeing him from the right and up close. A computer would not.

4. The neocortex stores memory in a hierarchy.

5. Hawkins proposed that the brain uses its stored memory to make predictions and calculations.

Regardless of the debate among neuroscientists, key for effectively teaching academic rules is to ensure that academic rules are remembered by the neocortex. Combining the contributions of Benjamin Bloom with modern-day scientists supports the need for teachers to engage their students in higher order thinking skills in order to create power for students' brains to more efficiently recall the information that was transferred (taught) to them.

Teaching pedagogy experts may recall *Synthesis* or the mental process we desire students to engage in to deduce from example or sets of facts. Whether neuroscience has determined that human brains "do not compute answers to problems" and that everything is pulled from memory" (Hawkins, 2004) should we abandon higher order thinking skills and higher order thinking questions?

Certainly not! Modern day neuroscience debates may have given us our best defense for the work that Bloom and others started decades ago. Chapter Seven and Power Source 3.0—*Transitions, Processes, and Endings for Learning* and Indicator 3.6—*Strategic Use of Higher Order Questioning* provide more details on the matter of Synthesis and other higher order thinking strategies for classrooms.

Inductive and Deductive Teaching

Inductive Teaching typically requires students to derive a definition (through inference) from examples provided by their teacher. Proficient teachers often direct guided practice to test the inference in some teacher-directed manner.

Deductive Teaching typically requires students to add to the number of examples similar to- or related to- those examples provided by the teacher supporting an academic rule or presented (taught) definition.

Standalone Discourse

- Academic rules without examples or non-examples

- Examples or non-examples without academic rules or concepts

70

Standalone Discourse often results when teachers are not mindful and/or planful on an intentional use of Inductive or Deductive teaching. When this occurs, *Standalone Discourse* is evident. **Power of Teaching** observers code a teacher's use of *Standalone Discourse* as ineffective with a left-side tally in Indicator 2.6—*Use of Standalone Discourse.*

Other forms of *Standalone Discourse* occur when concepts are provided without examples and are therefore standing alone and unproductive. Examples without academic concepts that are standing alone are almost always unproductive in the teaching and learning process. Academic concepts and principles in a taught lesson should have connected to them: examples, non-examples, guided practice, or active application attached to the presentation of the concept or material. Without these connections, Standalone Discourse occurs and should be coded as a left-side tally mark in Indicator 2.6—*Use of Standalone Discourse.*

Sample effective teacher behaviors for right-side coding in Indicator 2.6—*Effectively Applied Academic Rule with Examples*

- Teacher makes sure academic rules are stated, and ensures students understand how/when to apply the rules (or concepts)

- Teacher models application of academic rules (or concepts)

- Teacher points out academic rules when students use them

With data collected for Indicator 2.6—*Effectively Applied Academic Rule with Examples* the observer, when providing feedback to the teacher, will be able to assist the teacher to tap into one of the most well-documented but often overlooked component of effective teaching, that of matching academic concepts and rule with well-prepared examples and non-examples.

Remember the little guy from Chapter One who said to me, *"I believe she's rushing"* about his Kindergarten teacher? As I shared with you about that classroom visit, my observation was that the teacher *was* rushing. This little guy knew it. And he probably knew it was my fault, since I'd been expected earlier. We can *never* underestimate the perceptual abilities of our kids—even our youngest—when it comes to our teaching. What struck me most was the student's desire to explain that what I was seeing wasn't as good as Ms. Orb could be. He *knew* it. And he wanted me to know it.

Power Source 2.0—*Pacing & Productivity for Learning*, is a great source for teachers who seek to hone their craft when it comes to timing. Rarely do I think of this source of power for teaching and not remember, fondly, Ms. Orb and her work with her kindergartners back in 2004.

Notes:

Pacing and Productivity for Learning	Power Source 2.0
From *Power of Teaching* Observation Instrument	

INEFFECTIVE	TALLY	SUM	SUM	TALLY	EFFECTIVE
2.1 Missed Opportunity to Adjust Pacing When Needed					2.1 Use of Differentiated Pacing
2.2 Introduced New Concept/Activity-No Comprehension Check					2.2 Checked for Academic Understanding
2.3 Extended Discourse					2.3 Specific Dialogue to Excite Learning
2.4 Unproductive Remediation or Busy Work					2.4 Applied Grade Level Rigor
2.5 Indifferent Engagement of Students					2.5 Engagement w/Real- World Rigor
2.6 Use of Standalone Discourse					2.6 Effectively Applied Academic Rule w/Examples
2.0 TOTAL/RATIO	%			%	2.0 RATIO/TOTAL

2.1	Use of Differentiated Pacing

Look-fors and Listen-fors

Ineffective	Effective
Frustrated students who have insufficient time to finish their work	Teacher recognizes when students 'get it' and move on
Students are waiting	Teacher recognizes when students (or some students) need more time
Students have completed their work and teacher does not adjust pace	Flexible grouping
Teacher ignoring students' requests for a change in the speed of instruction	Modifications are made for individual students when necessary e.g., for students with learning disabilities, English Language learners, etc.

2.2	Checking for Academic Understanding

Look-fors and Listen-fors

Ineffective	Effective
Thumbs up, thumbs down indicators (for older students)	Thumbs up, thumbs down indicators (for younger students)
Teacher moves on too quickly without checking that students understand	A classroom where it is safe to say 'I don't know or I don't understand'
Teacher gives information without probing students' background knowledge	Teacher asks probing questions
Teacher moves on without establishing connections to what has been learned, or previously learned	Teacher has anticipated stumbling blocks to learning and scaffolds students
Blind adherence to program and/or pacing chart, with no comprehension checks	Multiple modes for checking used

2.3	Specific Dialogue to Excite Learning

Look-fors and Listen-fors

Ineffective	Effective
'Chalk and talk' lecture style teaching	Body language and vocabulary clearly communicate that the subject matter is interesting
Monologues	Explanations of why the subject matter is important
Focus on only a few students	
Teacher implies his/her own disinterest through voice/body language	Good range of teaching aides used (whiteboard, LCD, audio etc.)
Teacher overreacts to student behavior	No generalizations or vague language used
Teacher 'gushes' at students	Planned emphasis of key word and key concepts
Teacher's 'enthusiasm' is clearly forced/lacks authenticity	

2.4	Applied Grade Level Rigor

Look-fors and Listen-fors

Ineffective	Effective
Drill and kill	Work is at the appropriate grade level (or above) providing appropriate challenge to the students
Busywork	
Work that is too easy or too hard	Collaborative learning
Work that does not align with grade level expectations for the grade being taught	Students fully engaged
	Students regrouped as needed
Vocabulary that is too simplistic for the grade level being taught	Appropriate vocabulary and language usage

2.5	Engaging Students w/ Real-World Rigor

Look-fors and Listen-fors

Ineffective	Effective
Student indifference	Teacher ensures students understand the relevance, purpose, audience, application of what's being learned
Students are completing work out of compliance rather than engagement	Work is authentic
Work lacks rigor or any real relevance to the real world	Work demands problem-solving
Work has some real world relevance, but this is not explained to students	Students fully engaged
	Work goes beyond the textbook/program

2.6	Effectively Applying Academic Rule

Look-fors and Listen-fors

Ineffective	Effective
Opportunities to state and/or apply academic rules are not planned for or are missed	Teacher ensures that academic rule is stated, and makes sure that students understand how/when to apply them
Academic rules are referred to without checking that students either recall or understand them	Teacher models applications of the academic rule
	Teacher draws student's attention to academic rules when they state or apply them

Notes:

80

Chapter Seven
Transitions, Processes & Endings for Learning

Form over Substance = Beginnings, Transitions, & Endings

Form and Substance = Transitions, Processes, & Endings for Learning

--Joseph Wise, 2008
Edison Leadership
Development Academy

Transitions, Processes & Endings for Learning—is Power Source 3.0 leveraged in **Power of Teaching**. When students are turning on, turning off, attending to a lesson or moving from one lesson to another, these Indicators of effective teaching practice must be applied.

Beginnings, Transitions, and Endings of lessons are important to teaching. They are not in and of themselves dispositive of competent teaching; their power stems from a teacher's use- when strategic, they make concepts memorable. *Beginnings, Transitions, and Endings* are simply *tools* in the organization of teaching lessons—a means of placement for developing and clarifying for each student the content of a given lesson. Utilized at the surface level only, *Beginnings, Transitions and Endings* are insufficient or result in "form over substance." To achieve "form and sub-stance" well-planned, strategic *Transitions, Processes & Endings for Learning* must be actualized in a teacher's lesson.

Typically, researchers of teacher practices treat beginnings, transitions and endings of lessons as conventional markers—focused less on the *how* of kids' learning and more on the planning and timing of classroom activities. For decades school administrators have routinely (or incessantly, in some cases) examined lesson plans for content—inspecting for properly written learning objectives, advance planning of concrete activities, and frankly contemplating which teachers are exhibiting compliance with static standards (and which are not). Not infrequently, the inspection of lesson plans sometimes has been a convenient means to "document" under-performance by teachers perceived as ineffective or noncompliant (Hunter, 1984).

By way of example, I urge teacher educators and teacher leaders to build upon the work of Madeline Hunter (1984) who contributed mightily to our insights into lesson structure. An example of effective structure for teaching procedural knowledge—such as how to solve a problem in Mathematics--

you might remember Dr. Hunter's components of lesson design.

1. **Anticipatory Set**—A mental set that causes focus. Ex. *"Look at the equation on the screen and think about the rules we would employ to solve this equation."*
2. **Purpose and Objective**—students must always know when, what, and why they are supposed to be learning.
3. **Input**—Arrangement of activities for students to acquire new information, academic rules, or processes.

Ex. **K-W-L.** Lucy Calkins and other teaching experts espouse the K-W-L teaching model (Ogle, 1986) for driving instruction. Graphically organizing what we already **K**now, what we **W**ant to know and what we **L**earned as a result of the activity.

4. **Modeling**—showing students examples and non-examples by way of demonstration, or explanation.
5. **Checking for Understanding**—did students acquire the skill or new knowledge expected?
6. **Guided Practice**—student practice under direct supervision of the teacher.
7. **Independent Practice**—student practice without or with minimal supervision.

3.1 Making Lesson Transitions Explicit/Clear

Sounds simple, doesn't it? Almost like the track team's coach who advises a kid to "run faster" without offering her any idea as to *how* to do it. It's the same in teaching. Simply instructing educators to make lesson transitions clear does not in any way help them *make* lesson transitions have clarity.

Example:

Principal's directive to her teachers:

"Make sure you begin each new lesson with an explicit statement telling students that what you are about to do is distinct and new."

Resulting classroom comment by a teacher to his class:

"Class, last Friday, we completed the unit on invertebrates. Today we begin the study of vertebrates."

Is the example representative of compliant teacher behavior? Yes.

Is the example above representative of effective teaching? No.

What a principal should be advising and assisting with—and looking for when observing classroom instruction—is thought-provoking communication such as the following:

"Spinelessness has a couple of meanings, right? We know it sometimes signifies a lack of courage. But last Friday, we talked about *invertebrates*. Who remembers what that means? Who can identify at least three different invertebrates? . . . Now, let's talk about the *opposite* of what it means to be an invertebrate . . ."

Comparing and contrasting, a simple Venn diagram or any comparable strategy can be a straightforward way to introduce a new topic or lesson with clarity—and without Herculean effort. The point is to: (i) make it direct; (ii) make its newness unambiguous; and (iii) make the whole concept memorable.

Even an abbreviated version of making a transition clear might suffice as "effective" in Indicator 3.5—*Maintaining Academic Flow/Pacing*. Regardless, every transition must be marked and articulated as such.

If a teacher demonstrates a pattern of deficiency in Indicator 3.1—*Ineffective/Unclear Transitions*, or other patterns of ineffective behaviors for that matter, non-disparaging intervention is warranted during the feedback component of the process.

Sample effective teacher behaviors and student responses for right-side coding in Indicator 3.1—*Made Lesson Transitions Explicit/Clear* include the following:

- Teacher gives specific instructions for students
- Teacher reiterated instructions with clear and well-sequenced steps
- Teacher directed transitions are brief and planned activity begins quickly
- Teacher ensures students are starting quickly and on-task

Sample ineffective teacher behaviors and student responses for left-side coding in Indicator 3.1—*Ineffective/Unclear Transitions* include the following:

- Teacher doesn't help students understand connections among/between all assigned activities
- Dead space/time
- Lack of focus evident
- Students respond to bell rather than the teacher

3.2 Opening the Lesson or Topic with Clarity

When it comes to introducing a new concept, clarity is of pivotal importance. At no other point in a lesson is a teacher's role more significant—or more determinative of ultimate student outcomes relating to that concept. While we can observe and record a teacher's effective or ineffective verbal statements, we have to be mindful that *it's not just the words being said* that make a difference in teaching—it's *how*

83

they're being said. In addition to clarity of thought, there are verbal and nonverbal cues that have enormous influence over how students perceive—and retain—the message conveyed.

A review of the research revealed some basics that include the following:

- Vagueness often arises from a teacher's lack of subject area knowledge. (See also *Hiller, 1971*.)
- Defensiveness when students question fundamentals is often symptomatic of a lack of confidence.
- Sweeping statements and generalizations undermine the message—and impair what ultimately gets retained.

Notably, Smith (1984) examined the degree by which a teacher's poor word choices impair the learning process. Smith called them "bluffing phrases," and most educators have heard them at some point in their career:

Ambiguous Designation

Examples: *Some place*
Other people

Approximation

Examples: *Mostly*
Somewhat
Sort of

Indeterminate Quantification

Examples: *A few*
A lot
Some
Too many

Multiplicity

Examples: *Aspects*
Types of
Possibility
Perhaps
Maybe
Seems like

Probability

Examples: *Probably*
Sometimes
Infrequently

The bottom line is this: *Clarity* of instruction includes not just the *content* of what is taught, but the *way* in which it is taught. When we search for lesson clarity, we cannot simply inspect what's written in a lesson plan. Nor can we listen solely to the words recited by a teacher; we must look at the *how* of the lesson's total delivery. And that includes analyzing both the verbal and the nonverbal signals teachers—like all of us—send out every day, sometimes unwittingly.

Teacher clarity in communication is a pivotal factor in teacher success. *Clarity* is a *causal* factor in student learning. Its significance cannot be overstated: students hear but do not *learn* when the message is vague, hardly audible, or unbearably colorless. Although common sense tells us that, over decades we as educators have done little to confront our fundamental reality: A teacher's ability to communicate with clarity is not simply correlative to student learning. It is causal.

With respect to Indicator 3.2—*Opening the Lesson or Topic with Clarity*; Hiller (1977) Smith (1977) Smith & Edmonds (1978) Smith & Cotton (1980) and Smith & Land (1980) each demonstrated to statistically significant degrees, the effect of clarity of teacher communications on student performance (effective verbals—positive compared to vagueness—negative at correlations in the range of: from .001 to .05).

Sample ineffective teacher behaviors and student responses for left-side coding in Indicator 3.2—*Irrelevant Opening Activity* include the following:

- Students not engaged and lesson topic is ambiguous
- Teacher moving from topic to topic without identifying change or purpose
- Ineffective, worn-out routines
- Teacher does not explain the intended outcome of the activity

With data collected for Indicator 3.2—*Opened the Lesson/Topic with Clarity* the observer, when providing feedback to the teacher, can assist in further developing his ability to make learning explicit, and to provide ample anticipatory set for his students. This coaching can help the teacher to strengthen necessary mental transitions from one lesson or topic to another for students.

3.3 *Bell-to-Bell* Instruction

Bell-to-Bell Instruction is often viewed as a lofty or unrealistic goal. It is neither. The term simply means maximizing every minute of every school day, and utilizing the time we're given with our students most effectively. Historically, we've been pretty loose with transitional moments that are actually allocated for academic instruction—particularly at the beginning and end of each school day.

This issue brings to mind a classroom I observed in St. Louis: The teacher—with impeccable credentials and a heart for teaching—allowed more than 11 minutes at the beginning of her class to be squandered with unguided, unspecified student activity. This teacher was not uncaring or unmindful of academic needs—she was simply doing what a lot of us in teaching have traditionally done: assume that transition time means down time. But think about it: losing just 11 minutes per day (not hard to do) totals 55 minutes per week, or almost 4 hours per 20 school days. That's an astonishing 33 hours of instruction per year—more than a week's worth of school in most states—at each grade level. And that's *if* that child's teacher squanders only 11 minutes at the beginning of each day. Certain behaviors can make a difference:

Examples of <u>helpful</u> practices to maximize the *Bell-to-Bell* effect

- The teacher establishes learning *routines* for the beginning of each class or class period; these routines become almost ritualized in a sense; routines are patterns that students see as consistent, anticipated, and steadfast.

- The teacher *signals* that a class or new lesson is beginning. Simple phrases can establish the immediacy of a transition without it being jarring or disjointed i.e., *"Now* we're on to something new . . ." or "I need you to take out your journal and . . ." or "Let's put away . . . and go to . . ."

- Pace each lesson so that the bell ringing signifies the beginning or end of a lesson—a meaningful transition that is clear to students.

Examples of <u>unhelpful</u> practices that can negatively neutralize the *Bell-to-Bell* effect

- Taking attendance as a separate component of a lesson's start (Note: do not code this action as a right-side tally mark on the

Power of Teaching measurement tool). Routines for attendance-taking should be incorporated in a more value-added way as part of Power Source 3.0— *Transitions, Processes & Endings for Learning.*

- Building in "down time" at the beginning or end of a lesson. "Down time" is never meaningful—from an instructional or any other classroom perspective. *"It's almost lunch time"* or *"Pack up early"* are both signals that a teacher is shortchanging students.

- "Small talk" with students—talk that wanders from the lesson. (Not to be confused with *listening* and interacting in a personable way and steering off-point communications back to the lesson at hand).

Even though specifically causal teacher protocols and behaviors are measured on Indicator 3.3—*Bell-to-Bell Instruction*, the *intent* of the measurement is not to create a "gotcha" for teachers. Like the other Indicators comprising Power Source 3.0—*Transitions, Processes, & Endings for Learning*, Indicator 3.3— *Bell-to-Bell Instruction* is designed to help recognize often unwitting—and frequently overlooked—teacher behaviors and directions to students that interfere with instruction or create wasteful down-time. These teacher behaviors can be readily shaped and developed without a lot of fanfare, and without denigrating a teacher's efforts at engagement.

Sample behavioral evidence for effective (right-side coding) in Indicator 3.3—*Bell-to-Bell Instruction* includes the following:

- Brisk start
- Detailed directions
- Teacher moves around the room facilitating classroom productivity

Sample ineffective teacher behaviors and student responses for left-side coding in Indicator 3.3—*Downtime/Wasted Minutes* include the following:

- Slow/unclear start to lesson
- Inefficient distribution of materials
- Too much wait time (for students' attention)
- Wasted time
- Inefficient student and materials management
- Premature or unplanned end to lesson

So much focus on structures of classes and schedules, e.g. block schedules, 4X4 schedules, grade-level combinations, scheduling skinnies, pull-outs have caused us to skew our focus away from the actual quality and quantity of instruction once these schedules are all set. I am all for use of the schedule as an academic tool. Now is the time to adjust the balance between the structure and the

actual productivity within the structure. Helping teachers achieve the *Bell-to-Bell* effect by making each classroom minute productive is something we as instructional leaders attend to.

3.4 Providing for Relevant Academic Practice

In contemplating the importance of providing for relevant academic practice for students, we should start with a trap teachers often fall into—moving onto a new concept with no provisions for practice (ineffective Indicator 3.4—*Moved to New Concept w/No Practice*). Failing to provide relevant academic practice can be a common trap—particularly for novice teachers. Observers should be careful to measure and tally teacher-led discussion of a new concept; if opportunities for practice (relating to the concept) are not provided before the discussion moves on to other topics, intervention may be warranted.

An equally important and related issue for instructional leaders is to discern effective teacher protocols and practices codified as part of Indicator 3.4—*Providing for Relevant Academic Practice.* Over the past century, substantial research on homework's importance (relevant to driving learning and student achievement) has been inconclusive. Austin (1974) and Goldstein (1970) both documented assignment of homework as a positive correlate to achievement, but neither demonstrated a *causal* link between homework and achievement. Nevertheless homework remains a commonly accepted protocol for providing academic practice.

From the analysis Marshall conducted, **Power of Teaching** regards assigned homework in *problem solving* and *concept application* as causal factors to enhanced student achievement in Mathematics. Whereas in contrast, it is noteworthy that in at least one Marshall study (1983) overuse of arithmetic drill homework assigned for academic practice had a *negative* correlation to student achievement in Mathematics.

With **Power of Teaching**, classroom observers should *not* code the mere assignment of homework as an effective (right-side) tally unless the homework assignment is used as part of a review or other strategic reinforcement of the lesson observed or in preparation for the next learning experience.

Hovland (1938) established that *practice* is a causal factor in elevating student performance when teachers focus on the following factors:

- Varying in-class academic exercises with a mixture of practice activities (according to the teacher's strategic intent)
- Limiting the length of the practice on the basis of its complexity
- Scaffolding the practice activities at various levels of difficulty

It is common for teachers to move into questioning (Indicator 3.6) when providing relevant academic practice. Incumbent upon the observer is to move to 3.6 for coding and collecting measures of those behaviors. Data collection (classroom observation) is not a matter of the observer making instantaneous judgments. Assessment of the observed behaviors—along with providing feedback and coaching—come later.

Seatwork

Students of effective teachers do not spend more time in assigned individual work or independent study but the effective teachers behaved differently than those teachers evaluated as less- or ineffective (Medley, 1977). "When the effective teacher's [students] work independently, the teacher actively supervises them, giving careful attention to those individual [students] who, in the teacher's opinion, need it" (FPMS, 1989).

3.5 Maintaining Academic Flow/Pacing

Key to Indicator 3.4—*Providing for Relevant Academic Practice* (as well as Indicator 3.5—*Maintaining Academic Flow/Pacing)* is the question of how much practice is too much practice? Perhaps counterintuitive to many is the subject of math—lots of practice, using lots of math problems, is a good thing, right? Perhaps certain math pedagogy experts should partner with certain music pedagogy experts, who have long embraced the following:

Practice does not make perfect. Perfect practice makes perfect.

Practice requires purpose to be meaningful. It also requires pacing to ensure effectiveness. Most importantly, assigned practice should adhere to clear academic rules (Egan and Greeno, 1973). See related information in Chapter Six, Indicator 2.6—*Effectively Applied Academic Rule with Examples.*

Following are examples of helpful teacher practices that demonstrate teacher effectiveness in pacing and maintaining academic flow. When observed these should be documented as right-side tallies in Indicator 3.5—*Maintaining Academic Flow/Pacing*:

Helpful to *Maintaining Academic Flow/Pacing*

- Identifying for students what is about to happen
- Articulating concise and well-articulated directions
- Refocusing the group or class on a new topic or on multiple new topics in differentiated groups.
- Managing with fluidity a routine or ritual that involves a change in routine
- Providing a planned graphic organizer

- Utilizing a conference-style approach with students to handle certain individual student instructional interventions while assigning the whole class to other purposeful activities

Following are examples of impediments to maintaining academic flow and pacing. When observed, these teacher behaviors should be recorded as left-side tallies in Indicator 3.5—*Allowed/Created Fragmentation or Unproductive Discourse.*

Impediments to *Maintaining Academic Flow/Pacing*

- Enabling off-topic discussion from students without re-directing them
- Distributing materials with missing or incomplete parts
- Authorizing activities that have nothing to do with the lesson
- Personally engaging in discussion that is irrelevant to the lesson
- Providing garbled or insufficient directions to the students

Teacher Cuing

Cuing can be a powerful strategy to achieving more causality in Indicator 3.5—*Maintaining Academic Flow/Pacing* as well as in Indicator 1.3—*Questioning with Sufficient Wait Time* when a need to move the pace along is important.

Physical Education expert Rael Isacowitz (2006) formatted teacher cuing to student learning-style orientation. "Choosing the best type of cue for a [student] in a given situation speeds progress and makes the experience more fulfilling…"

Visual Cuing

Visual learners like to see a demonstration. "Offer a visual example… of the point that's being addressed. Execute an accurate and well-practiced demonstration. Your aim is to be a role model of what [is to be replicated or learned by the student.] For visual learners, there is a good reason to continuously practice the work and stay connected with the movements physically, mentally and viscerally" (Isacowitz, 2006).

Auditory Cuing

Auditory learners like an explanation, which might be analytical or figurative (imagery). Give a verbal explanation of the exercise or of the point that's being addressed. Develop ways to articulate the movements verbally. If the verbal cuing is based on the analytical approach, be sure the information is scientifically sound and the analysis clear.

If the cuing is based on a figurative approach, be sure the images make sense to the [student.] Imagery can be a very powerful tool when used skillfully, and most [auditory learners] respond well to this approach. An image creates a shortcut in the learning process, sometimes conveying in a sentence what would otherwise take a long time to explain.

Inappropriate imagery can be counter-productive (even when given with the best of intentions). Images that are not scientifically sound can sometimes create confusion. For instance, many a dancer has heard the cue, "lift the leg from the back." This image is intended to create an effortless, elongated movement. However, surely no one would dispute that the leg is not lifted forward with the hamstrings. The point here is that imagery can be based on concept or science—and both are legitimate—but a clear distinction should be drawn between the two to eliminate misunderstandings.

Experiential Cuing

Experiential (kinesthetic) learners like to do an exercise immediately. In this, a highly effective teacher might step back and let the process "happen." Allow the student to experience the movement or the point in discussion. Rather than bombard the student with corrections right away, allow a movement (or other learning) experience to take place. Once the student has achieved a basic understanding, corrections and directives can follow.

Tactile Cuing

Tactile learners prefer touch to sense the work. (Remember this comes from the Physical Education body of expert literature). Because touch is so direct and time efficient, tactile cuing is [a most valuable method of teacher cuing. However, owing to the nature of touch and its many possible implications and misinterpretations, great care should be taken when using this mode of cuing. Prior to using tactile cuing with a [student], it can serve well to mention its effectiveness in teaching and ask permission to use it, e.g. "M*ay I guide your arm through the routine?"* When using touch, be professional, deliberate and confident. If, however, a student appears uncomfortable with touch, choose other cuing methods (Isacowitz, 2006).

Power of Teaching classroom observers should look for another trap that novice educators frequently fall into—allowing more than one student to answer a question posed for one answerer. While a choral response may have some usefulness in limited circumstances, it is generally not an academic strategy that enhances student comprehension. (See also Indicator 3.4—*Providing for Relevant Academic Practice*, and Indicator 3.6a—*Differentiated/Strategic Use of Questioning.)*

A common trap that undermines instruction is the inelegantly-phrased—and often unintended—question that results in random, undisciplined and multiple student responses. The practice may not be harmful, but it in no manner empowers a teacher in ramping up his or her effectiveness.

Depending upon the context of a given lesson, the practice of allowing more than one student to answer questions posed should be coded as effective in Indicator 3.6a—*Differentiated/Strategic use of Questioning* or ineffective in Indicator 3.6—*Irrelevant/Overuse of Recall Questioning.*

3.6 Strategic Use of Higher-Order Questioning

Since the early 1970s, we have contemplated the use of questioning to reinforce learning, review lessons learned, and manage learners to encourage more time on task—and commensurately drive learner accountability. Kounin (1970) and Brophy & Putnam (1979) and numerous other scholars in more recent years have helped develop the use of questioning in academic instruction. Unfortunately, a trap for teachers persists: More time is spent using questions to keep learners alert and focused than on reinforcing a given concept i.e., teachers stating a question and *then* calling upon an unsuspecting—and off-task or daydreaming—student to answer. Using questioning as a technique may keep wary students on edge, but it doesn't always help to reinforce new concepts.

So much time and emphasis on using questions for behavior management (instead of concept-reinforcement) is unproductive and is a common trap for teachers. It also has a tendency to yield other undesired effects, including the spreading of inappropriate behavior problems to other students (See also Power Source 4.0—*On-Task Learning* in Chapter eight).

Marzano (2007) summarized research of Good & Brophy (2003) on the matter of treatment of student answers to teacher questions from students showing low evidence for high academic performance. Further research for *Power of Teaching* affirms these to be strong guiding principles for effective teacher treatment of responses from any/all students:

1. Demonstrate gratitude for students' responses
2. Never allow negative comments from other students.
3. Always point out what is correct and incorrect about the student response.
4. When a students is demonstrating difficulty, restate the question in a new way.
5. Provide ways to temporarily let students "off the hook."

Question Overload

When a teacher poses questions that are too long, too complex, or too ambiguous, "question overload" occurs.

Before the good and strategic *leveling* of questions can be mastered, clear and concise questions must be mastered. For example:

Negative Example—Teacher posed question relating to a lesson on JFK:

"At the location he chose, what type of building was used by the gun-man, was it in easy viewpoint for citizens to see, could the police and secret service have been better prepared; more alert?"

Effective Example—Teacher posed question relating to the same lesson:

"Can you tell me about the exact site the assassin chose to commit the murder?"

(Pause, wait time, react to the answer)

"Was this site in the building easily seen by police?"

(Pause, wait time, react to the answer)

"How about by the secret service and observing citizens?"

(Pause, wait time, react to the answer)

"Could officials have been better prepared? Why?"

92

(Pause, wait time, react to the answer)

A more productive and more strategic use of questioning arises when a teacher sequences inquiries at varying—and increasing—levels of engagement and difficulty. In education, we know this practice as *Higher Order Questioning*. But what exactly is meant by the term, and how does one know it when one sees or hears it? Bloom (1976) provided great clarity. The problem is, however, that when we refer to *higher order* thinking in teaching, we often fail to apply its richness to get the most strategic *power* out of teaching.

Questioning has to be a teaching and learning tool—not a behavior management tool. Some examples of common pitfalls for teachers in use of Questioning are outlined below.

Impediments to effective teacher use of Questioning include the following:

- permitting more than one student to respond at the same time
- two or more questions posed without a student response
- posing non-academic process questions, e.g. "Does everyone know how to put away their instrument?"
- posing general information questions, e.g. "How many of you went to the zoo on school-night-at-the-zoo?"

- posing simple questions requiring personal anecdotes without rigorous evaluative or other higher-order requirements.

Without a discernable strategic academic intent, each of these questions should be coded as Ineffective 3.6—*Irrelevant or Overuse of Recall Questioning.*

3.6a Questions Requiring Rote/Recall Memory

Definition of key terms:

Rote—*repetition of something so that it is remembered, often without real understanding of its meaning or significance* Encarta Dictionary (2008).

Recall—*to remember something or bring something back to mind* Encarta Dictionary (2008).

Although the practice of asking rote/recall/remembering questions is not harmful, there is consensus that they are rarely helpful in getting students to *think*. Except in times of academic warm up, or a need for a refresher, prolonged low level questioning of this nature has a tendency to expend time without developing significant academic growth. Because with limited use, such questions *can be* appropriate, below are some helpful stems that might be looked for when performing a classroom observation:

93

Helpful for identifying and crafting rote/recall questions:

- When did _____?
- Which one _____?
- Can you remember _____?
- Can you list four_____?
- How does the _____?
- Why did _____?
- Please select _____.
- How would you explain _____?
- What is _____?
- Who is _____?
- Who was _____?
- Can you recall_____?
- What is the definition of _____?
- What was the name of _____?

It should be noted that the fun of a fast-paced rote/recall-only regimen of questioning can be seductive—for both students and their teacher. These are common in Jeopardy-type classroom games and the practice of multiplication tables. Remember: the activities themselves are not per se harmful; they're just typically not helpful in powering up a teacher's teaching. Observers should watch for—and measure—the use of such questions. Preventing the overuse of questions through feedback and discussion can be enormously helpful to teachers (and ultimately, students).

Rote/Recall questions can be effective and can be coded as such in Indicator 3.6a—*Differentiated/Strategic use of*

Questioning so long as the observer can discern either the differentiation and/or the strategic intent of the teacher in using these lower-order questions.

3.6b1 Questions Requiring Analysis

Definitions of analysis:

Analysis—(close examination)—*the examination of something in detail in order to understand it better or draw conclusions from it.* Encarta Dictionary (2008).

Analysis—(assessment)—*an assessment, description, or explanation of something, usually based on careful consideration or investigation.* Encarta Dictionary (2008).

Questions requiring analysis or application (beyond simple rote/recall of facts) can be used as effective strategies to break up the cognitive monotony of lower level (rote/recall only) questions novice teachers often employ. These, as Bloom and replicators of his work note, are not higher-order. However, when used strategically, they can enable mastery of content. Code these as effective (right-side tally) in Indicator 3.6b1—*Required Student Analysis of Topic.*

Helpful stems for identifying and crafting questions requiring *analysis* include the following:

- What questions would you ask the author…?
- If he took the action of _____, what do you think would be the outcome?
- How would you _____, if you were in that position?
- What would you change in_____?
- In your mind, how would you organize_____?
- How would you show_____?
- Can you solve _____ a different way?
- How would you apply_____?
- What other way would you do to_____?

Wagner (2008) interviewed Mike Summers, vice president for global talent management at Dell, Inc. who stressed,"[t]here is so much information available that it is almost too much, and if people aren't prepared to process the information effectively [by way of analysis and reasoning] it almost freezes them in their steps."

Coding for effective teacher behavior (right-side tally) in Indicator 3.6b1—*Required Student Analysis of Topic* is appropriate when the observer witnesses the teacher asks and elicits responses from students in applying rules and properties, performing or applying steps in a process or creating alternative processes related to the lesson or topic.

3.6b2 Questions Requiring Academic Reasoning

Definitions of key term:

Reason—(verb)—*to consider information and use it to reach a conclusion in a logical way or to formulate or resolve something using rational means, e.g. to reason out a math problem* Encarta Dictionary (2008).

Reason—(noun)—*the power of being able to think in a logical and rational manner or the use of logical thinking in order to find results or draw conclusions or an argument or other example of logical thinking* Encarta Dictionary (2008).

Questions requiring academic reasoning often tap into the notion of creating—creating reasoned answers, alternatives, solutions, or new patterns—that use the knowledge transmitted. An example of reasoning could be application of an academic rule or concept.

Helpful stems for identifying and crafting questions requiring Academic Reasoning include the following:

- How would you adapt _____?
- Suppose you could _____?
- How would you test that hypothesis?
- Write (or) tell us your theory for _____?

95

- Tell us some things about _____?
- Draw or describe a model for _____?
- Please expound on your reason for _____?
- What would happen if _____?
- How did _____ improve upon _____?
- Are you thinking of an alternative to _____?
- How would you design _____?

Contemplating stems for questions requiring academic reasoning, Dr. Brenda Tanner also offered some powerful advice for *Power of Teaching*. Tanner suggests, that at times teachers will have the right idea—and desire to make student questioning more rigorous, but through perhaps a politeness will start the stem with "Can you…" Combined with one of the helpful stems above would be, "Can you tell us some things about____?" A student can simply answer *yes* or *no*. We should help teachers drop opening their questions with "Can you…" Simply directing the answer with "Please…" or another prompt will help teachers cause students to remain on-task and get to deeper thinking more quickly.

Coding for effective teacher behavior (right-side tally) in Indicator 3.6b2— *Required Academic Reasoning on Topic* is appropriate when the observer witnesses the teacher asking and eliciting responses from students in problem solving, creating solutions in new ways, explaining why, and/or applying an academic rule related to the lesson or topic.

3.6b3 Questions requiring Synthesis

Definitions of key term:

Synthesis—(noun)—*a new unified whole resulting from the combination of different ideas, influences, or objects; the process of combining different ideas, influences, or objects into a new whole.* Encarta Dictionary (2008).

Synthesis—(deductive reasoning)—*the process of deductive reasoning from first principles to conclusion.* Encarta Dictionary (2008).

Questions requiring synthesis from students are often those responses requiring parts-to-whole or whole-to-parts thinking or creating. These questions, when used well by the teacher, prompts students to move to a related but complementary or connected concept.

Helpful stems for identifying and crafting questions requiring Synthesis include the following:

- Identify the different components of _____.

- How did the story relate to
  _____?
- What inference can you make
  from _____?
- Compare and contrast
  _____.
- What was his motive for
  _____?
- Where is the evidence to support
  _____?
- What is the main idea of
  _____?
- Tell your pair/share partner the
  conclusions you've drawn from
  _____?

Wagner (2008) makes a strong case for teachers' use of questions requiring Synthesis. "For [organizations] to compete in the new global economy, they need every worker to think about how to continuously improve…products, processes, or services. The ability to think critically and apply what you know to new problems is also an essential skill for success in college."

Coding for effective teacher behavior (right-side tally) in Indicator 3.6b3— *Required Student Synthesis on Topic* is appropriate when the observer witnesses the teacher asking and eliciting responses from students in combining parts to create something new or making a whole from parts and parts from a whole in new and different ways related to the lesson or topic.

3.6b4 Questions requiring Academic Judgment

Questions requiring academic judgment often involve the facilitation of student value statements similar to or independent of the teacher's articulated value judgments. Questions requiring academic judgment often encourage students to state or develop, discuss and defend their viewpoint and the factors upon which they rely in forming that viewpoint. It is less common that a Mathematics lesson would generate questions requiring judgment. In Mathematics, similarly higher-order questions would require academic reasoning (Indicator 3.6b2) and not judgment (Indicator 3.6b4).

Helpful stems for identifying and crafting questions requiring Academic Judgment include the following:

- What choice would you have
  made? Why?
- How would you prioritize the
  issues…? How did you decide
  on your priorities?
- Would it be better had…
  happened differently? How so?
- How would you explain…?
  Why?
- Could you justify…? How?
- What made it better that…? Can
  you defend *your* position?
- Do you agree with the
  outcome…? Why? Why not?
- Why did she choose…?

97

- How would you compare the positions of _____ and _____?
- Determine and explain the significance of her _____.
- What evidence would you use to defend the position of ____?
- What is you opinion? Is that the point of view you first held? Why?
- What is behind your value judgment?
- What are the rules of engagement you think important? (for adolescents)
- What are the rules you think are important?
- Why do you think_____?

Coding for effective teacher behavior (right-side tally) in Indicator 3.6b4— *Required Student Academic Judgment of Topic* is appropriate when the observer witnesses the teacher asking students to evaluate and support, develop, discuss and/or defend a point of view related to the lesson, topic, or concept being taught.

Choral Response

Unison response to teacher questions and teaching prompts is viewed by some researchers, including Becker (1988) as effective when used appropriately. Becker provided that guided practice is warranted, unison response can be effective. Since the general focus on use of teacher-driven questioning is for causing students to think and to check for academic understanding in increasingly more rigorous ways, choral response should not be recorded as effective or ineffective in 3.6 Indicators. (See also Indicator 3.4—*Providing for Relevant Academic Practice.*)

Structural Alternatives (or Enhancements to Questioning)

Once strategic use of the various levels of questioning has been developed and fully embedded into a teacher's practice, then structural forms of such use is certainly enhanced. Providing teachers with certain structural formats such as *Think-Pair-Share* and *Ra-Ta-Ta* can enable teachers to direct students to share ideas and test their comprehension without using Questioning to check for academic understanding or to apply lessons learned, including academic rules.

Think-Pair-Share

Jodie Beckley, a colleague, instructional leader and General Manager with Edison Learning reminded me that she prefers to observe all students in a classroom engaged in contemplating and answering a teacher's questions. She believes, as many others do, that structures such as *Think-Pair-Share* should be observed for.

98

Think- Pair-Share

Think   Each student immediately begins to think on the teacher's question.

Pair   Each student turns to pair with a partner to,

Share   Share their respective thoughts before the class hears from one or more student a teacher prompted answer.

Ra-Ta-Ta

Ra   Read aloud
Ta   Think alone
Ta   Talk aloud

Advocates of the Workshop ritual/routine (ex. Reader's Workshop) advocate for structural enablers such as *Ra-Ta-Ta* for students to pair and work on teacher directed assignments.

These type of classroom rituals and routines should be incorporated; however, it should be noted that only when a teacher powers-up his practice with strategic use of higher order questions can this type of ritual/routine become powerful.

Schwenk & Whitman (1993) provide more guidance and defense for use of structural enhancers and structural alternatives to Questioning.

"During…teaching be prepared to encounter th[e more formative] stages of [student] development and the resistance that accompanies it, such as pressure by the students to tell them the answer rather than having them seek it on their own. As they advance "…students learn that…some judgments may be better or worse. We should always strive toward developing students to higher levels of development so that they reach "…the point of thinking that will prepare them to deal with personal and professional decisions—reasoning and analytical skills that …lifelong learners must possess." (Schwenk & Whitman, 1993).

With data collected for each area of Indicator 3.6—*Strategic Use of Questioning* the observer, when providing feedback to the teacher, will be able to assist the teacher to tap into one of the most under-utilized sources of power available to a teacher, that of leveraging strategically designed and effectively implemented questioning techniques known to be more causal to student learning and the transfer of knowledge.

Notes:

99

Notes:

INEFFECTIVE	TALLY	SUM	SUM	TALLY	EFFECTIVE
3.1 INEFFECTIVE/UNCLEAR TRANSITIONS					3.1 MADE LESSON TRANSITIONS EXPLICIT/CLEAR
3.2 IRRELEVANT OPENING ACTIVITIES					3.2 OPENED THE LESSON/TOPIC WITH CLARITY
3.3 DOWNTIME/WASTED MINUTES					3.3 *BELL-TO-BELL* INSTRUCTION
3.4 MOVED TO NEW CONCEPT w/NO PRACTICE					3.4 PROVIDED FOR RELEVANT ACADEMIC PRACTICE
3.5 ALLOWED/CREATED FRAGMENTATION OR UNPRODUCTIVE DISCOURSE					3.5 MAINTAINED ACADEMIC FLOW/PACING
3.6 OVERUSE OF RECALL QUESTIONING					3.6A DIFFERENTIATED/STRATEGIC USE OF QUESTIONING
					3.6B1 REQUIRED STUDENT ANALYSIS OF TOPIC / 3.6B2 REQUIRED STUDENT ACADEMIC REASONING ON TOPIC / 3.6B3 REQUIRED STUDETN SYNTHESIS ON TOPIC / 3.6B4 REQUIRED STUDENT ACADEMIC JUDGEMENT OF TOPIC — 3.6B STRATEGIC USE OF HIGHER ORDER QUESTIONING
3.0 TOTAL/RATIO	%			%	3.0 RATIO/ TOTAL

3.1 Making Lesson Transitions Explicit/Clear

Look-fors and Listen-fors

Ineffective	Effective
Students respond to bell rather than teacher	Teacher gives clear and specific instructions to student
Teacher responds to bell without providing a planned closure	Teacher ensures that all students understand instructions, reiterates them in sequential steps
Dead space/time	Connections are made between tasks/learning activities
Teacher launches into lesson activities without referring to previous learning or making connections with previous activities	Transitions are brief and focused
Students off task/unsure what they are required to do	

3.2	Opening the Lesson or Topic with Clarity

Look-fors and Listen-fors

Ineffective	Effective
Lesson topic/purpose is ambiguous	Teacher opens lesson/topic with enthusiasm, using appropriate vocabulary and demonstrating subject security
Teacher uses vague language possibly masking subject insecurity	
Learning objective is unclear	Opening activities are relevant and focused on learning objective
Teacher moves from topic to topic without making the change clear or explaining the purpose	Teacher scaffolds students as the introduction is made referring to previous learning and/or real world relevance
Worn out routines predominate	

3.3	*Bell to Bell* Instruction

Look-fors and Listen-fors

Ineffective	Effective
Slow/unclear start to lesson	Brisk, focused start
Inefficient distribution of materials	Detailed directions
Too much wait time	Moves around room, monitoring students' progress
Time wasted on ineffective student management techniques	Materials efficiently distributed
Premature end to lesson	Uses every instructional moment

3.4	Providing for Relevant Academic Practice

Look-fors and Listen-fors

Ineffective	Effective
Homework is busywork and/or finishing off incomplete assignments	Variety of activities strategically planned to practice what has been learned
Practice is too long often requiring unnecessary practice of a learned skill/concept with no new application, such as drill work	Length of practice is determined by the complexity of the activity
Teacher does not monitor students' responces sufficiently to ensure that incorrect procedures, algorithms, etc. are not being used	Practice activities are provided at varying levels of difficulty/complexity
No differentiation of practice activities to meet individual students' needs	Practice activities require problem-solving

3.5	Maintaining Academic Flow/Pacing

Look-fors and Listen-fors

Ineffective	Effective
Off topic discussions – either teacher or student led	Refocusing students when off topic comments are introduced by students
Incomplete materials	Providing clear, concise well-articulated directions
Explicitly or implicitly allowing off topic activities	Ensuring that students understand what is to happen next and how each section of the lesson relates to the other parts
Giving unclear directions, or insufficient directions to students	Using supportive tools such as graphic organizers
	Managing changes in activities with fluidity
	Managing students to enable them to adjust changes from established routines with ease

Notes:

Before advancing to Domain 2—*Managing Learners for Learning*, it might be wise to practice a bit with the following examples from Domain 1—*Focusing and Engaging Minds*. For each example of a teacher's teaching behavior, identify the Indicator (fill in the blank and (circle) whether the example is suited for an ineffective (left-side) tally or an effective (right-side) tally.

Observed Teacher Behavior

1. Teacher analyzed and presented material which led to students' acquisition of concepts.

    Indicator _____   **Ineffective – Effective**   **Left-Side – Right-side**

2. Teacher provided the meaning of a key term during the lesson without an example or further analysis.

    Indicator _____   **Ineffective – Effective**   **Left-Side – Right-side**

3. Teacher directed students in using a principle or law to solve a problem.

    Indicator _____   **Ineffective – Effective**   **Left-Side – Right-side**

4. Teacher specified an action, event, or object that stimulated students to evaluate the presented material.

    Indicator _____   **Ineffective – Effective**   **Left-Side – Right-side**

5. Teacher attended to a task and extinguished a disruption at the same time, and kept the lesson going all at the same time.

    Indicator _____   **Ineffective – Effective**   **Left-Side – Right-side**

6. Teacher kept students, as a group, focused on the work of reciting answers to her review questions.

    Indicator _____   **Ineffective – Effective**   **Left-Side – Right-side**

108

7. Teacher avoided an abrupt stop and kept the lesson moving.

 Indicator _____ **Ineffective – Effective** **Left-Side – Right-side**

8. Teacher provided several situations to help students apply the academic concept.

 Indicator _____ **Ineffective – Effective** **Left-Side – Right-side**

9. Teacher behavior indicated he was angry.

 Indicator _____ **Ineffective – Effective** **Left-Side – Right-side**

10. Teacher statement demonstrated empathy and amplified positive relationship to students.

 Indicator _____ **Ineffective – Effective** **Left-Side – Right-side**

11. Teacher engaged in multiple actions or talk beyond what was necessary for students to understand or learn how to participate in the group activity or use of classroom equipment.

 Indicator _____ **Ineffective – Effective** **Left-Side – Right-side**

12. Teacher behavior emphasized attributes that separated a family of concepts (e.g. executive branch, judicial branch, legislative branch) and encouraged students to reflect on the distinct attributes.

 Indicator _____ **Ineffective – Effective** **Left-Side – Right-side**

13. Teacher explained circumstances to which an academic concept applies.

 Indicator _____ **Ineffective – Effective** **Left-Side – Right-side**

14. Teacher directed students in determining that the correct rule was applied and solutions were properly reached.

 Indicator _____ **Ineffective – Effective** **Left-Side – Right-side**

Notes:

Chapter Eight
On-Task Learning

Volumes have been written and lectures abound on "managing classroom behavior." Teacher education course leaders persistently stress the serious need to keep students "on-task." The problem with much of the literature and intellectual property on all of this is the propensity to segregate student behavior from engagement in actual learning. Granted, a disciplined environment is important for students. But classroom orderliness is not in and of itself proof of effective teaching—and frequently can be evidence of the contrary. According to Jim Christensen, a school superintendent in Douglas County, Colorado, part of an on-task learning environment is "…an environment where children are [psychologically and] intellectually safe."

Having been kids ourselves, we all know in our gut a simple truth that resonates with common sense: Exciting, purposeful and focused activities in the classroom—and not simple rigidity—cause the greatest gains in academic achievement. Halting instruction to address behavioral issues can be on occasion necessary—but it *has* to be limited. A focus on classroom behavior in lieu of learning can be disastrous in the long term scheme of things. With respect to the involvement of students in the very classroom behaviors that students must display, a teacher's "meta-cognition, or thinking aloud about [the teacher's] expectations helps students understand [the] expectations as well as rationales for those expectations" (Tomlinson, 2005).

For centuries, educators have often embraced a common myth: anxiety is an awesome tool in behavior management. Playing on fear was perceived as not only a legitimate means to manage students, but a wholly appropriate one. Leading researchers have demonstrated that such practices are destructive—and reject them outright.

Unfortunately, not all teachers do.

Harsh discipline does, in fact, tend to create an orderly classroom environment—but at high cost. Students with learning disabilities, students with developmental limitations, and students who struggle are often lost over time, as they begin to reject the institution that they sense is rejecting them. In a CTAC study documenting their technical assistance for the Christina School District in Delaware (Slotnik, et al., 2006) one student's quote representing the sentiment of many high school students remains top of mind for me. "If the teachers teach better, the [student] behavior will improve."

Myth of the Value of Student Anxiety

Creating an anxiety-filled classroom or allowing anxiety to persist is more than simply unhealthy—it is the antithesis of what our profession is supposed to be about. And it's deadly if one's goal as a teacher is to facilitate a productive learning environment. Simply put:

> High student anxiety yields poor academic performance.

The more a child perceives her classroom to be threatening, the more her academic performance suffers. Some of the most important contributors to the literature on this issue made this reality clear decades ago. You may recall, for example, the work of Madeline Hunter—Remember Dr. Hunter's "levels of concern" when it comes to student performance on tests and projects? See also Cotler and Palmer (1970) Nottleman and Hill (1977) Kirkland and Hollandsworth (1979) and Zatz and Chassin (1985), who deepened our knowledge pool: "In classrooms that children perceived to be threatening, high…anxiety was associated with poorer…performance." Zatz and Chassin (1985) established certain predictability patterns (example: students with "unfriendly, boring teachers who have high expectations for student performance are more likely to [resort to] cheating.") Academic rigor - a highly valued component in *Power of Teaching*—is wholly inadequate without positive relationships with students.

Holding a teacher accountable for high academic expectations *without* commensurately looking at the effectiveness of his interactions with students is pointless. So here's an equation to ponder:

> Rigor w*ithout* Relationship Building = Ineffectual Teaching

Neither component can be examined in isolation: just as rigor is ineffective without a positive relationship between students and their teacher, a positive student/teacher relationship does nothing academically unless the relationship is grounded in rigorous academics. Consequently, ***Power of Teaching*** requires examination of both in unity.

4.1 Circulating and Assisting with Instructional Purpose

Circulating and assisting is not a new concept, and surely by now, we find few teachers who do not understand and implement this teaching basic known as *circulating and assisting*. A circulating and engaged teacher is a powerful enhancement to student engagement, student behavior, and student learning. To achieve more causal teaching and learning, we must develop our teachers to circulate and assist with instructional purpose. Skilled instructional leaders know when they are observing rote/routine classroom circulation vs. circulation and assisting with instructional purpose. Code these

112

behaviors on the left of the instrument (ineffective) or on the right-side (effective) in Indicator 4.1—*Circulating and Assisting with Instructional Purpose.*

Circulating and Assisting with Instructional Purpose has to do with many teaching tools and techniques. Circulating and Assisting is a means to an end and the end must be known and strategized-for on the part of the teacher. Like other Indicators, Circulating and Assisting has much to do with engagement.

Engagement

Engaging students in authentic ways can create power in several *Power of Teaching* Indicators. These include the following:

> 4.1—*Circulating and Assisting with Instructional Purpose*
> 2.5—*Engagement with Real World Rigor*
> 2.3—*Specific Dialogue to Excite Learning*
> 1.5—*Application with Real World Relevance*

Circulating and assisting with instructional purpose is another behavioral method to activate and validate the very engagement students must experience if any sort of learning is to occur.

Brandt (1998) provided compelling conditions for optimization of learning. These "best practices" offer observers evidence for a teacher's engagement of her students.

1. What a student is asked to learn must be personally meaningful.
2. What a student is asked to learn must be challenging and the student accepts the challenge.
3. What a student is asked to learn must be appropriate to the student's developmental level.
4. What a student is asked to learn must be orchestrated so each student learns in his own way, with choices, and feels in control.
5. When a student is asked to learn, she must be required to use what she already knows to construct the new knowledge.
6. Successful learners have opportunities for social interaction.
7. Successful learners get helpful [and timely] feedback.
8. Successful students are required to acquire and use strategies.
9. Successful students experience a positive emotional climate that supports the intended learning. (Brandt, 1998)

4.2 Redirection/Disciplining in Private

"Higher achievement is attained in classrooms that function under higher

113

teacher direction" *Crocker & Brooker (1986).* In analyzing behavior management and standard-setting efforts of teachers seeking to attain higher achievement in classrooms, Crocker & Brooker discovered a common teacher practice that was rarely questioned: a failure to adjust behavioral interventions when forceful direction proved inadequate.

Although it strikes many as counterintuitive, *ignoring* inappropriate behavior has been demonstrated to be highly effective in multiple circumstances (Madsen & Madsen, 1998). But let's face it: ignoring misconduct is not a one-size-fits-all strategy. Neither is applying specific academic praise a one-size-fits-all strategy. Regardless, when used effectively and suited to individual students levels of readiness and maturity, ignoring inappropriate behavior and applying specific praise have been proven remarkably effective at redirecting behavior in a variety of circumstances. (*See also Indicator 4.5- Applied Specific Academic Praise.*) On occasions when simply ignoring an act is itself inappropriate, or when it is simply ineffective, the *how* of intervention becomes pivotal. *How* does one reach a kid who appears intent on disturbing or disrupting, and still keep others engaged?

There are no easy answers, and no prescribed scripts. Often, success has as much to do with the *tone* of the teacher as it does with the words expressed.

Here are a couple of sample responses to a disruptive student that I've observed effective teachers use (the success of which, of course, depends on the dynamics of each specific circumstance):

- Pause. Look at the student directly and calmly state "You and I need to talk. We're going to do that"—and *immediately,* without missing a beat, turn away and resume the lesson (the implication being that you will address the conduct with the student, but privately, and only *after* you complete with the class something far more important). By immediately turning away/back to the matter under discussion, the teacher limits a natural tendency for things to escalate—it no longer is a confrontation. The maneuver also enables the student to maintain a little dignity, sometimes reducing his or her need to demonstrate defiance.

- If the behavior is attention-seeking and disruptive, *immediately* engage the student personally in the lesson itself in *any* way possible. As an example, during a discussion of *To Kill A Mockingbird,* I witnessed a student drawing attention to himself in a disruptive way. The teacher immediately acted as if the student's behavior was somehow relevant and said to him "Right!

That's probably something like those kids were thinking. But now let's say you're Boo Radley. In your own words, tell us why you stayed in that house so long. What motivates a guy to do something like that?" The key, as the teacher explained later, was to "haul disrupters into" the topic—firmly but respectfully. The teacher went on, "I just want to convey the message that *their* take on any issue I'm raising is of intense—and genuine—interest to me."

- If you sense the disruptive student is deliberately attempting to provoke a negative response from you (and let's face it, for a variety of reasons, that is often a primary motivator for some students), there is a natural tendency to respond viscerally. *Avoid visceral responses at all cost; emotion in reaction to baiting behavior is deadly.* Instead, feign mild amusement—treat the behavior dismissively and move on, even if the disruptive behavior is not wholly eliminated. Once the lesson is completed, *then* apply face-to-face discussion—but privately.

Obviously, these limited tactics are samples and would apply to only certain scenarios. However, the point they make is this: *Phrasing* is often not nearly as important as the tone being set. Firmness in private (privacy to the maximum extent possible) with a crisp reprimand is the most widely proven strategy for positive results when simply ignoring or redirecting the inappropriate behavior doesn't work. Direct correlations have been demonstrated on this issue over time:

- There is a statistically significant correlation between loud/angry reprimands and probability that the misbehavior will spread to other students who had not been misbehaving (O'Leary, 1970.)

- A direct correlation has been demonstrated between "group alert" (loud group reprimand or redirection) and inadequate student achievement. (See Brophy & Putnam, 1982 for example.)

- Even though firm tone, and authoritative direction with disruptive students should be considered as effective teacher behaviors, positive outcomes in *on-task learning* will not be achieved through anxiety producing direction, redirection, or instruction (Bauer, 1975).

4.3 Making Student-Centered Meaning with Examples and Non-Examples (Stand-Alone Discourse)

For achieving and sustaining instructional benefit from Power Source 4.0—*On-Task Learning* and also positively affecting other Power Sources (including 2.0—*Pacing and Productivity for Learning* and 3.0—*Transitions, Processes, & Endings for Learning*) stating concepts with a definition followed by supporting examples and non-examples grouped (or sequenced) together were powerful. This power is amplified by teacher explanation on why or why-not each example or non-example was related to the concept or definition being taught. (McKinney, Larkins, Ford, & Davis, 1983). Concept teaching supported by well-chosen examples and non-examples are more powerful with immediate subsequent guided student practice. Guided student practice should also be coded as a right-side (effective) tally in Indicator 3.4—*Providing for Relevant Academic Practice.*

The work behind Florida Performance Measurement System (1989) documented another power behavior in the use of linking words when treating concepts and definition with well-placed examples and non-examples, especially when cause-and-effect relationships are being taught. Considering this with those researchers providing guidance on effective use of verbals/nonverbal and accentuation on the linking word provides more power for teaching and learning. (See also Indicator 1.1—*Effective Verbals/ Non-verbals*.)

Tennyson, Youngers, & Suebsonthi (1983) found that examples are more important (powerful) than critical attributes in concept understanding and retention. Frayer (1970) provided that students who were given fewer good examples did just as well in learning concepts as those students who received more examples. Frayer documented four (4) as *fewer* and eight (8) as *more*. A teacher droning on with more than a few well-developed, well-articulated examples or non-examples should have their effective behavior documented and then the extended behavior documented as being negatively neutralized and therefore ineffective as a left-side tally on Indicator 4.3—*Academic Concepts without Examples/Non-examples.*

Example of a positive (and accentuated) linking word:

"If sodium chlorite (liquid chlorine) is combined with ammonium hydroxide (household ammonia), **_then_** noxious and potentially lethal fumes are created.

4.4 Advanced Sorting of Materials

What at first glance strikes most of us as trivial is in fact surprisingly crucial: The manner in which we as teachers sort and manipulate materials for students. Ironically, a simple failure to plan for the mundane parts of our work can impair even the best of lessons.

Some positive examples of what to look for when observing teacher practices on this issue include the following:

- Counted stacks of hand out material by rows or tables for students prior to class beginning
- Queued video to specific points germane to the lesson or academic concept being worked
- Warm-up or *Do Your Own* activity pre-posted on white board or electronic media board for students to engage as they take their places in the classroom
- Lab equipment already prepped prior to the class arriving

The observable benefit from these examples is straightforward: organization of materials preserves each minute of time for teaching and learning, rather than distracting from it. *On-Task Learning* is a Power Source and organization of the tools being used can have a make-or-break effect on the lesson itself. Less apparent is the equally powerful benefit of materials organization mastery itself—so that manipulation of peripherals and resources becomes unnoticed, and secondary to the actual focus of lesson. (FPMS, 1989).

Certain causal teacher protocols and behaviors are crucial in effective teaching—and need to be measured. Materials management (coded in Indicator 4.4—*Advanced Sorting of Materials)* is no exception. For example,

is pausing to write information on a whiteboard effective teaching? How does it compare to having the information already in written form before the lesson begins, i.e. in the form of a handout or overhead image-projection? Valuable time—and momentum—are often lost when teachers interrupt a lesson to set up a lab or projector, or pause to count or distribute materials during instructional time. Any loss of instructional energy due to handling of materials—if the handling could have been more efficiently done beforehand—is worth noting. Constructive coaching at these times becomes important. Effective time management has a direct impact on the overall operation and climate of the school.

4.5 Applying Specific Academic Praise

The power of *specific* academic praise to enhance cognitive development has been established through traditional teaching pedagogy and through extensive neuroscience. (See also Chapter Five). In addition to solidifying an individual student's memory of a concept, there is also less-documented benefit: when authentically earned, specific praise affects not only the individual student but the entire class as a group. In a nutshell, specific and authentic praise tends to enhance an aura of winning as a "team." For this reason, it is recommended that *Appl[ying] Specific*

117

Academic Praise in **Power of Teaching** is observed for in two different and distinct impacts—impact on the individual, and impact on the group.

As already observed and revealed by so many experts in our field effective use of praise is paramount for effective teaching. (See also Chapter Five— Power Source 1.0—*Cognitive Connections for Learning* and Indicator 1.6—*Applying Specific Academic Praise*.)

FPMS (1989) provided the following guidance on effective use of teacher-delivered student praise:

1. Effective praise is delivered contingently—on correct and desired responses—and <u>never</u> when the praise was not warranted.
2. Effective praise specifies the particulars of the accomplishment.
3. Effective praise suggests clear attention to a student's accomplishment- often with spontaneity, or other forms of authenticity.
4. Effective praise rewards achieve-ment of specific performance criteria.

Missed opportunities to administer proper and effective praise should also be an ineffective (left-side) tally in Indicator 4.5 or in Indicator 1.6.

4.6 Stopping Misconduct Strategically

Working on behavior management and classroom control is something we routinely focus on as educators—and it's what raises the highest anxiety in new teachers. But despite our focus on behavior control, we frequently miss the mark. We've learned that parental-type intuition rarely works in a classroom setting—at least, in classroom settings involving inappropriate or disruptive student conduct. Consequently, when we talk about powering-up teaching in Power Source 4.0—*On-Task Learning,* we must think strategically about group dynamics. And we need to use what works.

O'Leary (1970), Madsen & Madsen (1998), and Kounin (1970) established that inappropriate behavior is diminished in environments involving warmth and the perception that the adult in the room "liked" students. But warmth and demonstrative "liking" does not eliminate unacceptable behavior—it tempers it. Highest level of behavior management have been attained, it turns out, when task-focused techniques accompany warmth and acceptance. Further, undesired "cascading" effects of misconduct on other students are radically reduced. For example, Madsen & Madsen clarified that in multiple circumstances, ignoring certain negative behavior and a just-in-time acknowledgement of positive behavior in other learners provides a "redirecting" effect.

O'Leary's work (1970) also demonstrated that the notion of the "soft reprimand"—understated/calm comment without direct eye contact—can be powerfully effective (direct eye contact can divert other students' attention away from the lesson and towards what they perceive as potential teacher/student conflict). O'Leary's work demonstrates that disruptive behavior gets redirected more readily by "soft reprimand" than by loud or more confrontational efforts—or by group-as-a-whole reprimands.

Roughness is associated with aggression; the rougher a teacher's tone or words to a member of a group, the greater the behavioral disruptions in that group tend to become over time. Further, as students reach adolescence, harsh or course interventions actually become viewed as a challenge—and in today's more litigious environment, kids are savvy enough to know that when confronted with a persistently shouting or bombastic teacher, they're dealing with a paper tiger. Harsh words legally cannot be followed up with harsh action—nor should they be. But historically, the threat of physical punishment is what shouters had relied on when their shouting led to escalated misbehavior. It was wrong then, and it is wrong today.

So what can a teacher do when kids in a group lack basic civility—when they seem wholly unconstrained by fundamental rules of respect for themselves and others? The answer is: it depends. The age and dynamics of the group, and the relationship the teacher is developing with those in the group are pivotal factors. One thing is certain, however: displays of anger by a teacher don't work.

O'Leary (1968) observed that even kindergartners who witnessed a punitive or angry redirection by a teacher most often responded with escalated behavioral disruption. According to colleague Tom McDowell, respected national special education and curriculum expert, this is especially true too for students with certain learning-related disabilities.

Kounin's work demonstrated that when high school students witnessed teacher anger, roughness, or perceived unfair handling of a behavioral issue, they viewed the teacher as having poor judgment and lacking capacity to handle the class. One of the most profound studies on the issue of teacher response to disruptive behavior (O'Leary, 1968) involved first-graders: in that study, students became demonstrably more concerned about aggression and conflict and less concerned with academic matters as a teacher escalated the use of punishing roughness and/or anger.

We have a clear picture of what doesn't work. The harder job is describing what does. Here are a few contrasting examples that may help when it comes to redirecting behavior for Power Source 4.0- *On-Task Learning:*

119

Helpful

"This is critical stuff—listen for a moment to this: _____ ."

Not Helpful

"Stop chatting right now."

Helpful [To a meandering student who has gotten up while others are continue working]:

"I need you to be seated so we can work on this . . ." (softly, without anger, and as minimally distracting to other students as possible under the circum-stances).

Not Helpful

"I don't like you leaving your seat without permission."

Helpful

"In a moment, I am going to be calling on one of you to lead us through the answer to this question."

Not Helpful

"Shhh, Shhh. Listen."

Helpful

"Remember, you are to only use the calculators after you solve the first three problems."

Not Helpful

"Hey, what do you think you're doing?"

Helpful [privately]:

"Mary, it's wrong to grab others' supplies without first asking. I'd like you to go apologize to Jermaine."

Unhelpful

"Class, no one should be taking things from others without permission."

Concluding Remarks

While our team's research clearly led us to advocate for the tight integration between managing student behavior and maintaining the academic momentum of a lesson, nothing in *Power for Teaching* refers to behavior management or behavior modification outside the classroom or learning environment. Our research applies only to effective teacher practices and maintaining on-task behavior in the classroom.

INEFFECTIVE	TALLY	SUM	SUM	TALLY	EFFECTIVE
4.1 Circulated with Explicit Purpose or Remained at Desk					4.1 Circulated & Assisted w/Instructional Purpose
4.2 Group Chastisement/ Consequences					4.2 Redirection/ Disciplined in Private
4.3 Academic Concepts without Examples/ Non-examples					4.3 Made Student-centered Meaning w/Examples or Non-Examples
4.4 Counting/ Sorting Materials on the Fly					4.4 Advanced Sorting of Materials
4.5 Use of General Praise					4.5 Applied Specific Academic Praise
4.6 Delays Behavior Management					4.6 Stopped Misconduct Strategically
4.0 TOTAL/RATIO	%			%	4.0 RATIO/ TOTAL

4.1	Circulating and Assisting with Instructional Purpose

Look-fors and Listen-fors

Ineffective	Effective
Sitting at the Desk	Circulating the room, checking that all students are successfully engaged in the set task
Standing by the board/window watching	Strategic interventions to ensure that the learning flows
Wandering around the room without purpose	Subtle redirections that do not interrupt other students
Giving all/most attention to one or two students	
Interrupting the learning when a student is engrossed (except when you can see they are on the wrong track!)	
Interrupting the whole class to redirect one student	

4.2	Redirecting/Disciplining in Private

Look-fors and Listen-fors	
Ineffective	**Effective**
Group Work	

4.3	Making Student-Centered Meaning with Examples and Non-Examples

Look-fors and Listen-fors

Ineffective	Effective
Teaching points made with no associated examples or non-examples	Clear examples/non-examples provided to illustrate teaching points
Too many examples offered reducing student interest	Key words or linking words used to accentuate relationships
No practice of concept offered	Explanations as to why – or why not an example demonstrates the teaching point
	Guided practice is provided

4.4	Advanced Sorting of Materials

Look-fors and Listen-fors

Ineffective	Effective
Handing out papers one by one around the class	Pre-sorted and collated materials in strategic places for easy distribution
Students having to leave seats unnecessarily to locate regularly used resources	Regularly used resources easily accessible
Teacher leafing through textbook to find place	Places in textbooks tabbed for easy location
Writing a 'do now' as students enter the room	Instructions pre-written on board for starting activities
Fast-forwarding or otherwise searching for the right spot on electronic media	Media cued and ready for use

Applying Specific Academic Praise

Look-fors and Listen-fors

Ineffective	Effective
'Good job' 'Class, I am so pleased with Deiondre' 'Well done!' 'Nice work, Noah' 'I am so proud of Rosario'	'Good job Kevin, you used the skip-counting method to add in your head.' 'Deiondre, you should be proud of yourself. You remembered to conjugate the verb when you drafted your response.' 'Wow! Rosaria you read that passage very clearly, enunciating all the consonants so crisply!'

Chapter Nine
Differentiated Teaching to Accelerate Learning

Proficiency for all kids is not an aspiration. We must aspire to something more for all kids.

> --Matt Chapman,
> NWEA Chief Executive reflecting on the global achievement gap work of Tony Wagner

Proficiency and beyond is something to which we must be held accountable. To get there acceleration is required. To accelerate learning, differentiated teaching must occur.

Before school leaders can fully address Power Source 5.0—*Differentiated Teaching to Accelerate Learning* for all kids, there first must be an established definition of what is meant by *differentiated instruction*. **Power of Teaching** advocates the definition provided by the National Center on Accessing the General Curriculum (NCAC) as a foundation on which to build classroom and organizational capacity around *Differentiated Teaching to Accelerate Learning*. Tracey Hall, Senior Research Scientist for NCAC documented the following definition.

To differentiate instruction is to recognize students varying background knowledge, readiness, language, preferences in learning, interests, and to react responsively. Differentiated instruction is a process to approach teaching and learning for students of differing abilities in the same class. The intent of differentiating instruction is to maximize each student's growth and individual success by meeting each student where he or she is, and assisting in the learning process (Hall, 2002).

Callahan (2004) noted that "unfortunately, many administrators opt for a differentiated instruction model without a full understanding of the conditions that must be in place for effective implementation." Researchers and those who are masters in teaching compel us to think of powerful differentiation in terms of five key behavioral components:

- Activity grouping
- Use of classroom furniture
- Use of multiple-adults
- Use of data amplifying academic concepts, and
- Emphasis on salient academic points.

For administrators and other instructional leaders who are proficient in observing classroom instruction for these Indicators, it is critical to: (a) disclose issues that are observed (b) offer suggestions if improvement is needed, and (c) hold teachers appropriately accountable for differentiation in the classroom (Strickland, 2004). Strickland asserts that on-going sharing of "how" must include "on-going sharing of results" relating to a teacher's efforts: "To be an effective support to teachers there must be provided a balance between *seeing the light* and *feeling the heat*."

Eric Smith, Commissioner of Education for the State of Florida, a trusted colleague and important mentor shared great wisdom about his experiences with teachers and the misguided views novice teachers often hold about differentiated instruction. Dr. Smith explained that so many times teachers view differentiated instruction as simply needed-remediation for some kids or lower standards for certain groups of students. This conversation with Dr. Smith about Power Source 5.0—*Differentiated Teaching to Accelerate Learning* reinforced the finding of Hall (2002) that first and foremost a school system, a school, or a faculty team at a school must be resolute about what it means to differentiate teaching and to differentiate instruction. For sure differentiation must accommodate individual needs of students to catch-up (not stay behind) or accelerate (through extra- or what I call turbo-work) so that other kids can be helped by the teacher where catch-up might be needed. Caution must be taken to ensure that teachers, even unwittingly,

must not pretend to differentiate when in-fact all they are accomplishing is to contain some kids into an academic "cage" of low standards or low expectations from which they cannot escape.

Another powerful case for increasing opportunities and skill for teachers to differentiate is made by Tomlinson (2005). Tomlinson's compelling reasons include the following:

1. Because students have different backgrounds and interests, there is no guarantee that they will all find the same things personally meaningful.

2. Students learn at different rates, so a particular pace, text, or activity challenges some students while frustrating or boring others.

3. While some students are thinking more concretely others are processing more abstractly. At the same times students will be more independent while others are dependent.

4. "It's a sure bet students won't all opt to learn in the same way, make the same choices, or feel in control with the same parameters."

5. Since students don't all bring the same knowledge to the lesson and do so with varying degrees

128

of competency, they will construct knowledge differently.

6. Learners vary in the amount of peer collaboration they can manage and need. The type of peer learners they work with is another variable to successful learning.

7. Helpful feedback for one student is not necessarily similarly helpful to another.

8. Students need to acquire and utilize learning strategies in ways that are personally helpful.

9. Classrooms that are positive for some learners can be "distinctly not so for others."

10. Students need varying degrees of activity scaffolding to achieve learning goals.

Power Source 5.0—*Differentiated Teaching to Accelerate Learning* provides teaching behaviors, classroom protocols and rituals and routines that enable effective differentiation for all students. Nothing in Power Source 5.0 within *Power of Teaching* alone can guard against what some have called the soft bigotry of low expectations for some still held by some teachers and some schools. Russlyn Ali, Assistant U.S. Secretary of Education refers to the soft

bigotry of low expectations as "not so soft." That sort of bigotry must be dealt with through values clarification and values reconciliation among educators working together.

5.1 Strategic Activity Grouping

Those who have led us to think in more *causal* ways about the use of activity grouping in powering up a teacher's teaching, know that "classrooms in which students are active learners, decision makers and problem solvers are more natural and effective than those (classrooms) in which students are passive recipients of information" (Strickland, 2004).

As *Power of Teaching* is utilized to develop masterful and more causal teaching behaviors, it is wise to ensure that a teacher's use of flexible group differentiation shows evidence of consistent and purposeful grouping. When purposeful grouping is consistently used, students benefit to an even greater degree than from other power sources. The practice of effective differentiation also enables deeper results from Power Source 4.0—*On-Task Learning*.

Flexible grouping should be used often and with consistent practiced rituals and routines. Strategies for flexible grouping are essential. Learners should be expected to interact and work together as they develop knowledge of new content.

129

Teachers may conduct whole-class introductory discussions of content big ideas followed by small group or paired work. Student groups may be coached from within or by the teacher to complete assigned tasks. Grouping of students is not fixed. "As one of the foundations of differentiated instruction, grouping and regrouping must be a dynamic process, changing with the content, project, and on-going evaluations" (Hall, 2002).

For more novice teachers who need to begin mastering the art of differentiation through flexible grouping, Tomlinson (2005) suggests use of an "anchor activity" to help free up the teacher to be able to focus on the students and their needs. "Ragged time is a reality in a differentiated classroom... inevitably [some students] complete work, while others have more to do." Anchor activities "that are options for students after assigned work is completed at a high level of quality" should be part of the protocols used in the differentiated classroom.

Tomlinson (2005) also asserted that "tim[ing of] differentiated activities to support student success" must be mastered for effective and more-causal teaching through differentiation and flexible grouping. For teaching success the teacher should "remember two things: (1) time allotted for a task should be a bit shorter than the attention span of the students who work on that task, and (2) advanced learners often have extended attention spans."

With data collected for Indicator 5.1a—*Flexible Groups for Accelerating Learning* the observer, when providing feedback to the teacher, will be able to assist the teacher to tap into one of the most widely discussed but too often poorly utilized strategies—that of activity grouping. To effectively power-up a teacher's classroom, activity grouping must become widely used and used well. Experts such as Hall (2002) Tomlinson (2005) and Strickland (2004) have provided us with strong research and documentation to understand the causal nature of well-managed activity grouping.

When teachers plan through a "strong rationale for differentiating instruction based on student readiness interest and learning" evidence of their mastery will become evident to the observer (Tomlinson, 2005).

5.2 Strategic Use of Furniture to Flexibly Group

One of the most important aspects of strategic use of classroom furniture is that the physical arrangement provide for organizing students in flexible ways. This flexibility can provide instructional, interactive, physical, visual, and aural advantages to the teacher's lesson or activity that yet again powers up the classroom practice. Marzano, Gaddy, Foseid, and Marzano (2005) concluded

130

that there are typically several components to consider:

1. Access to learning centers and equipment (including technology)
   a. Number of centers?
   b. Primary patterns of traffic and movement?
   c. Centers closed or open?
   d. Lab or project materials?

2. Decoration and general arrangement of the room to include use of walls, empty space, and artifacts (going beyond a simply "print rich" classroom).
   a. Affect upon entering the room?
   b. Strategically used wall space or simply busy walls?
   c. Will all students be able to see and hear when necessary?
   d. Lighting (naturally and artificial)?

3. Materials and equipment on hand —quantity, quality, and organization.
   a. Safety and first aid materials?
   b. Music, projector, player equipment and extra bulbs and cords?
   c. In/out box, student portfolio, running records, guided reading

and project materials and arrangements?

4. Student and teacher and chairs, music and speaker stands and lecterns, and the teacher work area(s).
   a. Whole group and small group work areas?
   b. Safety planning?
   c. Storage areas?
   d. Will all students be able to see and hear when necessary?
   e. White board and projector screens amply located for viewing?

Tomlinson (2005) added aptly to this list of critical components.

5. Assign students into groups or seating areas smoothly.
   a. Calling individual names to move is "bulky, and confusing" and is a time-waster. Use of colors, wall charts, or projected maps are among the most respected and well-documented practices in managing these types of classrooms.
   b. Younger students typically need more carefully arranged protocols than older students; however, older students may need more careful assistance in tracking the usefulness of

131

the group moving to their learning.

   c. Ensure protocols minimize stray movement of students. Assignment of certain roles among the students can lend value to a teacher's craft in assigning students to groups and stations.

6. Have a "home base" for students.
   a. Allows for checking attendance in secondary schools without calling the roll
   b. Beginning and ending from a home base arrangement can allow for orderly and efficient organization of materials (see also Indicator 4.4—*Advanced Sorting of Materials*).

7. Teach students to rearrange the furniture
   a. Students should know the floor plan
   b. Be clear about expectations for orderly movement
   c. Show students the value-add for doing the rearranging

8. Engage students in classroom procedures and grouping processes

   a. Ask students how well they are doing when they move to small groups
   b. Be open to student's solutions—they can some-times see them before we do.
   c. Students should co-own all classroom processes and protocols

Rist (1970) found that teachers typically seat those students for whom they have low expectations of succeeding farther away from the front or to the most frequent places of instructional action. Developing teachers should be made aware of this as a warning, so as to avoid being "typical".

Keith, et al (1974) found that increased use of the blackboard [whiteboard] tended to coincide with increased irrelevant [undesired] student behavior. FPMS—Florida Performance Measurement System (1989) designers asserted, based upon Keith's work, that developing teachers must be trained to learn how to effectively use [whiteboards] as a "positive emphatic technique...without creating a classroom management problem..." This finding has overlapping relevance to Power Source 4.0—*On-Task Learning*, and Indicator 1.1—*Effective Verbals/Nonverbals*.

Use of classroom furniture and equipment (including chalkboards and dry-erase whiteboards) should be coded as effective or ineffective in Indicator 5.2—*Use of Furniture to Flexibly Group;* however, inappropriate student behavior should be coded as part of Power Source 4.0—*On-Task Learning* (as a left-side tally).

5.3 Strategic Use of Multiple-Adults to Enable Differentiation

Among my colleagues first in Delaware and later in many states, many effective practitioners contemplated and developed the *Team Approach to Mastery* (TAM) as a way to schedule, organize and team adults with children, mostly as a way to better integrate students having special education service needs with peers who did not. As this practice evolved, it became evident that the TAM and similar co-teaching arrangements are easily transferrable to multiple educational settings, and is effective in scenarios broader than special education inclusion.

Especially when square footage of a single classroom is sufficient, having multiple adults (licensed teachers and paraprofessionals) with students— arranged with suitable tables/desk/furniture layouts—sharply enhance instructional opportunities. (See also Indicator 5.2—*Use of Furniture to Flexibly Group* in Chapter Nine.)

Teaming multiple adults with well-defined roles can power-up many of the elements of differentiating teaching.

5.4 Strategic Use of Data to enable Differentiation & Flexibly Group

Progress Monitoring has become a widely-discussed educational practice. Making Progress Monitoring actionable and meaningful is a far more difficult thing to do than simply talking about it.

Protocols for use of data to power-up flexible grouping arrangements and teaching flexibly grouped students were found effective when managed in 6 phases by the Washington state-based Technology Alliance in 2005. These six phases are outlined below:

Phase 1. Establish desired outcomes. Teachers (and sometimes students) discuss and define criteria for what constitute satisfactory outcomes. Questions during this activity may include: What do we want our students to know and be able to do? What standards will be used to judge success?

Phase 2. Define the questions. What questions do we have about our learning environment? Examples include: What do we want to know about our students? Why is one group of students performing better than another? Are these strategies improving comprehension?

Phase 3. Collect and organize data involves gathering evidence needed to answer the questions asked. Much of the data typically exists in various forms, including exams, essays, observations, and formative and summative test data.

Sometimes it is just a matter of locating and using existing data. Other times, teachers may decide that new data must be generated to answer the questions. Some questions to ask during this phase: What kinds of evidence/data suit our needs? Where can we find the data? Can these data be disaggregated into groups? Will we be able to manage and interpret this data or will it require additional expertise or software to assist with the analysis?

Phase 4. Make meaning of the data. Raw data is rarely ever useful. Data collected must be put into context and understood as a whole before any conclusions can be made. Patterns, relationships, unexpected out-comes, are all possibilities once a close reading of the data is conducted. The most important component to this phase is making sure the right questions are being asked.

Phase 5. Take action after data has been collected, organized, and interpreted. The challenge for a school or classroom teacher is to take action to improve student learning based on what the data reveal. Teachers and schools may do everything from changing teaching methods, curriculum supplements, schedules, classroom layouts, to the extremes of creating new programs or reorganizing the entire school focus. Without taking action, the inquiry cycle is pointless.

Phase 6. Evaluate and assess actions. At this point, the cycle essentially begins again. The new actions, that came about from the previous phase, need to be analyzed to determine if the actions and changes have had an effect on student learning. Thus, outcomes need to be determined, questions identified, data collected, etc. (from the Inquiry Cycle, Technology Alliance, 2005)

Use of data also has much to do with providing students timely feedback on their performance data. "Frequent feedback is particularly beneficial to learners from poor educational backgrounds and to students demonstrating little motivation" (FPMS, 1989).

"Once [a teacher has] data about student learning progress…" there must be a planned response to the data. "If students seem to be learning well, the teacher [can proceed with] broadening or deepening students' understanding. …if the data indicates that there are students experiencing difficulty, the teacher may find it necessary to stop and reinvent the lesson or provide students with additional time for [guided] discussion and questions (Carter, 2009).

Use of data to enable differentiation pertains to both the differentiating for individual student needs as well as differentiating the pacing for small groups or large groups of students.

5.5 Accentuated Responses with Linking Words

Rosenshine (1975) documented strong positive correlation between teacher use of linking words and student achievement when explaining new ideas, concepts, or information. Linking words powered up the explanation and comprehension. *Power of Teaching* researchers advocate that linking words and phrases should be accentuated through the teacher's voice inflection and articulation.

Examples of helpful <u>Linking</u> words/phrases:

- *therefore*
- *thus*
- *then*
- *so that*
- *in order to*
- *consequently*

Similar to the teaching power that strategic use of examples, non-examples, and definitions provide in Indicator 4.3—*Mak[ing] student-centered meaning with examples or non-examples* the use provides equally to teaching power in amplification of academic concepts and could also be coded in Indicator 5.5. When carefully executed, students are more likely to learn and retain concepts and theories that are more difficult or complex by their teacher making strategic use of definitions, examples and non-examples. Anderson (1972) found this in college-age learners. Johnson & Stratton (1966) found this among grade school age students. Further evidence of the power of examples, definitions, and non-examples was documented by Tennyson (1973), Tennyson (1978), Feldman (1972), and Klausmeier (1976).

5.6 Emphasizing Salient Academic Points

Teaching mastery includes effective handling of salient academic points to ensure they are absorbed and learned by students. Giving enough clear information in varied manners so that students discern whether an object, idea, or event belongs to (or is separated from) a family, category, or class is basic, but necessary. Emphasis of salient points can be achieved by strategic repetition, strategic changes in the speed of speaking, and/or in the differentiation of examples and clarity provided to different learners based on the teacher's checking for academic understanding. (See also Indicator 2.2—*Checked for Academic Under-standing.*)

Summary

As Cindy Strickland (2004) relates the power of differentiation, she sometimes shares a little story from a masterful teacher she knows:

"There was a time in my classroom when it was all about sculpting young lives in the shape of their singular dreams, to become what makes them whole. And at that time, in my classroom I understood it was not my classroom, but ours—our place to find ourselves in books, and query, and in one another..."

To early adopters of differentiation, there appears a tendency to think in terms of individualization. There are times that individualized instruction is appropriate and best, and on those occasions it's important that it be used. Often, however, a teacher's students' performance data indicate the need for flexible grouping and differentiation in small groups—as opposed to individualized instruction. Masterful teachers know too how to individualize learning and learning activities without simply thinking of individualizing as 1 on 1 instruction. Practical individualizing is rarely achieved 1 on 1.

Once observers collect data and are ready to assist teachers-- especially more novice or less-skilled teachers, to increase their teaching dexterity with more causal behaviors to facilitate and accelerate learning, great skill and care must be used by the observer in providing feedback and developing the teacher. Teachers should be asked to begin differentiation at a comfortable pace. "Some teachers already make frequent adjustments in...instruction to allow for student differences in their classrooms." These teachers must simply add to and build upon their craft with tweaked guidelines. Other teachers "need to move in smaller increments" (Tomlinson, 2005).

As Power Source 5.0—*Differentiated Teaching to Accelerate Learning* is mastered, Tomlinson's (2005) wise-counsel should be considered: "[like their students, some teachers] leap like lizards through a given task, others move at a more measured gait. What matters most is that students—and teachers— make more progress from their respective beginning points, not that they all work alike." Dr. Strickland's teacher-friend's insight also resonates: For effective teachers it is all about *"our"* classroom—not *"my"* classroom.

Notes:

From *Power of Teaching* Observation Instrument

INEFFECTIVE	TALLY	SUM	SUM	TALLY	EFFECTIVE	
5.1 Missed Opportunity for Activity Grouping					5.1a Flexible/Groups for Accelerating Learning	5.1a Flexible Grouping for Accelerating Learning
					5.1b Strategic use of Heterogeneous Grouping	
					5.1c Strategic use of Homogenous Grouping	
5.2 Under-utilized Classroom Furniture					5.2 Use of Furniture to Flexibly Group	
5.3 Under-utilized adult(s) to enable learning					5.3 Use of Adult(S) to Flexibly Group	
5.4 Under-utilized achievement/ Activity Data					5.4 Use of Data to Flexibly Group	
5.5 Ignored Student Engagement/ Responses					5.5 Accentuated Academic responses or Amplifies Academic Concept	
5.6 Glossed-Over Pertinent Academic Operations					5.6 Emphasized Salient Academic Points	
5.0 TOTAL/RATIO	%			%	5.0 RATIO/TOTAL	

137

	Flexible Grouping for Accelerated Learning	
5.1		

Look-fors and Listen-fors

Ineffective	Effective
Desks arranged so that rearrangement is difficult	Use of colors, maps, charts to reassign seats
Walls that 'scream' or 'whisper' instead of 'talking'	Clearly established routines for regrouping for assigned tasks
Charts, whiteboards, screens etc difficult for all students to see	Unobtrusive and efficient rearrangement of furniture when necessary
Teacher positioned in such a way that actively monitoring students is difficult or impossible	Resources easily accessible and well organized
Chaos results when students regroup due to lack of planning and routines	Strategic placement of teacher/media to ensure effective communication
	Wall space and artifacts used well to support learning

5.2	Strategic Use of Furniture to Flexibly Group

Look-fors and Listen-fors	
Ineffective	**Effective**
Desks arranged so that rearrangement is difficult	Use of colors, maps, charts to reassign seats
Walls that 'scream' or 'whisper' instead of 'talking'	Clearly established routines for regrouping for assigned tasks
Charts, whiteboards, screens etc difficult for all students to see	Unobtrusive and efficient rearrangement of furniture when necessary
Teacher positioned in such a way that actively monitoring students is difficult or impossible	Resources easily accessible and well organized
Chaos results when students regroup due to lack of planning and routines	Strategic placement of teacher/media to ensure effective communication
	Wall space and artifacts used well to support learning

139

5.3	Strategic Use of Adult(s) to Flexibly Group

Look-fors and Listen-fors

Ineffective	Effective
Additional adults standing at edge of room/sitting at desk disengaged	Additional adults work seamlessly with teachers facilitating learning
Additional adults completing mundane tasks	Additional adults clearly understand their role in the lesson
Additional adults working with students but clearly do not understand lesson objective	Additional adults are clearly well-briefed and understand the learning objective
Additional adults interfere with the learning process	

5.4	Strategic Use of Data to Flexibly Group

Look-fors and Listen-fors

Ineffective	Effective

Group
Work

141

5.5	Accentuated Academic Responses with Linking Words

Look-fors and Listen-fors

Ineffective	Effective

Group
Work

5.6	Emphasized Salient Academic Points
	Look-fors and Listen-fors

Ineffective	Effective

Group Work

143

Notes:

Chapter Ten
Aligned Expectations to Macro-Organization

[T]he school transformation process is creating a shared vision throughout the organization of what a school looks like when no child is left behind.

--Lisa Carter, 2008 on
Instructional Alignment

Once I had completed my first 280 classroom visits as the new school superintendent in Wilmington, DE I distributed a memo to all teaching and leadership staff. In addition to summarizing the themes I had observed, the memo also described what I was seeking for the future:

1. **Deep engagement in the most rigorous levels of the content. Every single day with every single student.** *If you and I cannot see it in the brightness of their eyes then the students are not deeply engaged. By "brightness of their eyes," I mean the excitement that we see in children when they are grasping new concepts or ideas. Despite some outstanding examples, I did not see overwhelming numbers of students with brightness in their eyes in the 280+ classroom visits. It would make me exceedingly proud to see this on my second round of classroom visits this year.*

2. **Differentiated activities designed to leverage the talents, accommodate the weaknesses and improve the productivity of every learner.** *In many classrooms and in a majority of the TAM classrooms I visited, I was struck by missed opportunities to adjust, mix and vary activities between and among teachers, paraprofessionals and students. To best reach, challenge and task learners in effective and rigorous ways, we need to differentiate classroom activities much more than we previously have attempted. I'm hopeful that by my second round of classroom visits, we'll have developed multiple practices that — although possibly less conventional than in the past — will be actively engaging students in creative and differentiated ways.*

145

3. ***Productive (verbal and non-verbal) "noise" is great!*** *We all learned classroom control when honing our craft as teachers. I will look forward to our District becoming a national model for demonstrating the fine balance between controlling for the sake of control and facilitating for maximum productivity of our learners.*

4. ***Precision is imperative.*** *Every missed opportunity to model precision in all content areas and in our use of the English language — and to not expect that precision from our students—is a missed opportunity. I look forward to a significant increase in the precision we demonstrate in content, curriculum and the English language in all our classrooms.*

5. ***Positive, professional and persistently punctual learning environments*** *must become the norm in Christina School District. My evidence includes many sightings of positive, professional and persistently punctual classrooms. I can always tell these within seconds of arriving in a classroom because there is a crispness in the air. In these instances the teachers are assertive and positive, the room is in productive, physical order and*

every minute of instructional time is filled with instruction and not "filler" activities. There are many classrooms where this is <u>not</u> the norm. I will look forward to seeing <u>much more</u> of this "crispness" in the weeks and months ahead.

6. ***Research-proven use of academically-specific praise, redirection and interaction.*** *Now is the time to increase the frequency of these powerful tools. Praise, redirection, questioning and other teaching interactions are powerful instructional strategies when rooted in or extended with specific academic reinforcement.*

7. ***Feedback – We all need it to maintain and enhance our performance.*** *That goes for us all! I continue to seek feedback from you on what I'm doing, and I urge you to seek the same from others close to your teaching practice. I also encourage you to give feedback to other teachers, as well as to other employees, students, and parents. When we seek and/or provide feedback that is candid, well-intentioned, psychologically safe and well timed, it becomes the most powerful tool for improving performance. I'm asking everyone—teachers, administrators, and all, to engage in the feedback process.*

146

This is especially critical if you have direct responsibilities that closely influence the student learning process. Principals and Assistant Principals, I expect your leadership to provide more opportunities for all sorts of productive feedback to those close to the teaching/learning process in every Christina School District classroom.

(Excerpts of memorandum to certificated staff, Christina School District, January, 2004)

This memorandum certainly was not in-and-of itself a guide for effective teaching; it served merely as a message about our need for both consistency and constancy and was reflecting the role of the Superintendent in impacting learning- through the same system.

Subsequently we worked hard on our own and engaged the technical assistance of CTAC—Community Training and Assistance Center—to enable us to: (i) probe for more causal factors preventing the achievement of some students in some classrooms and (ii) align our work in and among all classrooms.

Substantial and worthwhile work over the past 20 years has enabled better aligned district-wide, school-wide, and grade-level practices. Whether you are a centralized-oriented instructional leader (and believe that all work has to be aligned from the top of the organization downward) or whether you are a more decentralized-oriented leader, one thing should be clear: alignment of curriculum to standards, assessments and lessons is powerful—and crucial to our practice. In recent years we have learned too that common-assessments, common-planning, professional learning communities, adherence to a central curriculum, academic standards and fidelity to consistent implementation *all* influence academic achievement. Power Source 6.0—*Aligned Expectations to Macro-Organization* is offered to strengthen effective alignment within each teacher's practice.

Power Source 6.0—*Aligned Expectations to Macro-Organization* is also suitable for collecting other types of evidence of effectiveness, including and beyond observed teacher behavior. Tally marks should be used in the same manner as previously utilized (one entry for each observance of an effective or ineffective practice—this time relating to instructional alignment among the district, region, school, department or grade level). Five categories (Indicators) are specified in *Power of Teaching;* three more remain available for further and specific customization.

6.1 Appropriate Materials in Full Use

There are a lot of good materials out there to support our work i.e., *America's Choice* technical assistance or the *Frank DeSensi Group* for aligning instructional

147

strategies and unpacking standards. *Edison Learning's* School Design and Alliance model and Synesi Associates' school turn-around technical assistance are used in many states and in the United Kingdom. The work of leveraging of Professional Learning Communities, and the use of common assessments among teachers are also used. The list of technical assistance providers is extensive and exhaustive.

Where we often fall down—after studying and attempting to install all of these and other potentially powerful materials and contributions—is in the implementation. Although we like to speak about *fidelity of implementation, sustainability, and constancy,* our actions don't always match our words. Worse, these same words: *Fidelity of implementation, sustainability, and constancy* along with others have become buzz words and phrases to the point that we cannot even hear them anymore, let alone sufficiently contemplate their meaning.

"What gets measured, gets done" (Peters, 1987)—and commensurately, that which we don't measure tends to fall through the cracks. Put in terms of our profession: What the school principal says is important—and models for others as important—and will likely be evaluated or scrutinized on a regular basis.

Historically, we have not *measured* how our classroom teachers implement and use the very materials we have painstakingly adopted. Until now. Indicator 6.1—*Appropriate Materials in Full Use* and other Indicators in this Power Source 6.0 are designed to examine implementation of (and fidelity to) what a team has—together—decided works.

6.2 Teacher Arranged Artifacts In-Use

Teacher-made, purchased, or other visual classroom aids ("artifacts") have come a long way since those green alphabet displays we had for generations—remember them, draped across the tops of chalkboards in virtually every American classroom? For decades, they *did* serve as visual aids that assisted thousands of children to learn both print-writing and cursive penmanship. In recent years, however, we've learned a lot more about classroom stimuli, and the way visually compelling artifacts may reinforce lessons. We've also learned that generally, classroom artifacts are a *correlative*—not causal—factor in raising student academic achievement. Although memory gems, the display of student work, and other visual classroom enhancements can make a classroom "print rich"—and *that's* certainly not a bad thing—we need to look farther when we're observing all that affects learning. The bottom line is this: physical attractiveness of a classroom can *influence* learning—it does not cause it. Classroom observations must go well beyond physical appearances—the major premise behind *Power of Teaching.* Consequently, Indicator 6.2—*Teacher Arranged Artifacts In-Use* is provided to solely record the strategic use or lack of visual aids—nothing more. Artifacts can positively influence learning and they can establish means by which we know whether learning is occurring. Artifacts do not replace powerful teaching behaviors.

6.3 Strategic Use of Relevant Student Performance Data

Every district, region, school, department, and grade level should have clear protocols governing the use of student data—and student data can include all sorts of things: records of progress monitoring, formative assessments such as Measure of Academic Progress (MAP) by Northwest Evaluation Association, NWEA), use of DIBELS data, PSAT performance data and item analysis, statistics arising from commonly-developed faculty assessments, and more.

When examining data and the manner in which it is collected, it is critical to probe for *alignment* to curriculum and *linkage* from classroom to grade level to district academic goals. See also Indicator 5.4—*Use of Data to Flexibly Group.* Sometimes, data is collected and compiled solely because it has always been collected and compiled—not because it assists us in differentiating

instruction, or in meaningfully influencing individual student's learning anomalies. For these reasons, meaningful use of data is a component of what gets measured in *Power of Teaching*.

Colleague Tom McDowell also made a bold and thought provoking statement to me when he reviewed Power Source 6.0—*Aligned Expectations to Macro-Organization*:

"Joey, this [data collection and data reporting] is really over-kill in some schools and school systems. In some places it is data for sake of data and no one knows anything but a score. In many places, we aren't using data for the benefit of kids. We often use data for adults to look good and to argue over irrelevant issues."

(See also Indicator 5.4—*Use of Data to enable differentiation & flexible group.*)

6.4 Teacher Arranged/Displayed Student Work

We also know—more now than ever before—about the strategic use of classroom walls, bulletin boards, and even hallways to post and display student work. Indicator 6.4—*Teacher Arranged/Displayed Student Work* is provided to enable observation and analysis of how an individual teacher may use designated hallway space to create extensions of his or her classroom. (See also Indicator 6.2—

Teacher Arranged Artifacts In-Use.) Again, it should be noted that artifacts—in a hallway or elsewhere—continue to be a component of learning environments; they are not, however, dispositive of *effective* teaching. Indicator 6.4—*Teacher Arranged/Displayed Student Work* is provided to record for strategic use of classrooms and hallways as an element of teaching—not as proof of teaching effectiveness, but as evidence of thoughtful teaching strategies.

Again, McDowell provided caution about the use of displayed materials and student work:

"This is very important and is forgotten today. Too often it is not student work, but bought stuff."

Kindergarten Student Writing as Back-to-School Welcome

Quick story: I loved visiting schools, especially on the first day of each academic year. When visiting schools in Jacksonville, FL in 2006 on the first day of school with Barbara Langley, one of my highly-regarded staff members, we encountered a great practice implemented by one of her region's elementary school principals: Kindergarten Student Writing as a Back-To-School Welcome.

Elementary school is a special place on the first day of school, since so many very young children (often with very young parents) are separating for a whole day without much separation experience. For Kindergarten or Pre-Kindergarten families, there are special temporary spaces like the *ya-hoo-boo-hoo* room for shedding tears, taking pictures, and resolving unexpected meltdowns. There is typically a great deal of welcome-back-to-school decoration and paraphernalia.

This particular principal, with her teachers, had forgone use of any traditional welcome materials and posted work from their prior year to excite parents and students about the work to be done in this new school year. At the front door of the school was a wide bulletin board with last year's kindergarten class and their writing samples from the beginning of the year with writing samples from all the way until the end of the year. Imagine those new Kindergarten parents I observed who were in awe over what it was going to be like to watch their child progress from September, to November, to February, to March, to May.

Barbara convinced more of her region's principals to lead welcome-back-to-school rituals in this same strategic way in subsequent years.

Displaying student work in classrooms and in other areas of the school, when done strategically, can provide

150

significant power for teachers and teaching.

6.5 Grade-level Endorsed use of Word Walls and Word Wall-Type Devices

Word Walls and word wall-type devices have their place in effective teaching— no one disputes that they can assist in developing high-frequency words or deeper, richer vocabulary. But the mere existence of a Word Wall does not establish teaching effectiveness; like any other artifact, it is an environmental enhancement that does not, and cannot alone, trigger academic gains. Indicator 6.5—*Grade-level Endorsed use of Word Walls* is provided solely to record the use of a certain type of visual aid designed to buttress vocabulary growth. (See also Indicator 6.2—*Teacher Arranged Artifacts In-use.*) Although much has been published—especially by certain textbook and basal publishers— about effective use of Word Walls, the bottom line remains the same: A Word Wall is an artifact. Nothing more and nothing less.

That said, please note that Word Walls can positively affect classroom environments and hence, when used properly, can positively affect learning. That's why Word Walls and word wall-type devices are included in *Power of Teaching.* When aligned to a documented, aligned teaching strategy, Word Walls can constitute evidence a

substantive teaching practice, which should be recorded as a right-side *Power of Teaching* tally in Indictor 6.5— *Grade-level Endorsed use of Word Walls,* when observed.

Customizing Indicators 6.6, 6.7, and 6.8

Indicators 6.6, 6.7, and 6.8 are provided for customization; these open items are designed to enable teachers and principals to identify and record teaching practices aligned to agreed upon (and documented) goals at the grade, departmental, school, region, and district levels, as appropriate. Space beneath each Indicator is provided to insert customized—yet fully aligned— practices.

Possible Customized Indicators for schools and school systems are listed below:

- Use of displayed Positive Behavior Support (PBS) data or incentives agreed upon in a school's or team's plan
- Strategic use of a math word wall agreed upon in a school-wide math team's or school's plan
- Strategic use of agreed-upon elements of Reader's-Writer's Workshop
- Observing for fidelity of treatment of a prescribed literacy series or program that teacher

151

have been trained to use effectively

- Strategic use of warm-ups or do-your-own activities for the beginning of class that have been agreed upon by a team, a school, or a school system.
- Alignment of classroom Protocols to districts response to Intervention processes
- School-wide focus on specified writing activities
- _____
- _____

Notes:

INEFFECTIVE	TALLY	SUM	SUM	TALLY	EFFECTIVE
6.1 Unrelated Busy-work Materials in Use					6.1 Approved Materials in Full Use
6.2 Non/Misused/Under-Resourced walls					6.2 Teacher Arranged Artifacts In-Use
6.3 Non/Ineffective-Use of Student Performance Data					6.3 Strategic Use of Relevant Student Performance Data
6.4 No Student Work Posted					6.4 Teacher Arranged/Displayed Student Work
6.5 Non/Misuse of Word-Walls					6.5 Grade-level Endorsed use of Word-Walls
6.6					6.6
6.7					6.7
6.8					6.8
6.0 TOTAL/RATIO	%			%	**6.0 RATIO/TOTAL**

153

6.1	Approved Materials in Full Use

Look-fors and Listen-fors

Ineffective	Effective

Group
Work

6.2	Teacher Arranged Artifacts In-Use

Look-fors and Listen-fors	
Ineffective	**Effective**

Group
Work

6.3	Strategic Use of Relevant Student Performance Data
	Look-fors and Listen-fors

Ineffective	Effective

6.4	Teacher Arranged/Displayed Student Work
	Look-fors and Listen-fors

Ineffective	Effective

Group
Work

157

6.5	Grade-level Endorsed use of Word-Walls

Look-fors and Listen-fors	
Ineffective	**Effective**

Group
Work

6.6	
Look-fors and Listen-fors	
Ineffective	**Effective**

Group
Work

6.7

Look-fors and Listen-fors

Ineffective	Effective
Group Work	

6.8	

Look-fors and Listen-fors

Ineffective	Effective

Group
Work

Notes:

Chapter Eleven
Systematizing *Power of Teaching*

"Calling on teachers to change their practice invites them to experience 'the humiliation of becoming a raw novice at a new trade after having been a master craftsman at an old one."
-Kauffman in Evans, 1996

In this chapter, we should—together—contemplate leveraging *Power of Teaching* as a system for teacher-to-teacher, and teacher-to-instructional leader partnerships. This collaborative effort can be achieved through one-on-one and small group sessions. At its core, systematizing *Power of Teaching* requires a clear and demonstrable respect for the work of teachers; it also requires recognition of the enormous demands all in education face. Maximizing teaching effectiveness isn't about imposing speculative demands on teachers—nor is it about setting abstract performance targets. It is about exploring what works, and what doesn't, for each of them in the classroom. *Power of Teaching* works only if it is implemented in an organizationally healthy manner; it is intended to maximize what teachers do for their

students. If used improperly, it can undermine the very core of a teacher's strengths.

As had been discussed earlier, effective use of *Power of Teaching* requires the measuring and contemplation of an individual teacher's ratio of effective-to-ineffective teaching practices and behaviors so that consciously increasing the ratio of effective practices can persist. This is done by focusing on more *causal* factors—teaching behaviors that have been documented to drive to learning and retention) rather than on *correlative* factors (behaviors that may *correlate* to a healthy learning environment but do not in-and-of-themselves trigger understanding, comprehension, and learning). Through this behavioral focus, teaching effectiveness is enhanced; enhanced effectiveness advances student academic achievement.

As already discussed, the State of Florida has used a similar system of teaching practice analysis known as the Florida Performance Measurement System (FPMS). Like *Power of Teaching*, FPMS involves direct observation of teaching practices, data collection on those practices, and delineation of specific behaviors that are effective or ineffective. Danielson's *Frameworks of Teaching* and Resnik's *Lenses of Learning* also provide ways of analyzing worthwhile teaching practices. All of these efforts reveal that "unhelpful" practices are not actually harmful or damaging to children per se

163

(unless, of course, such practices involve unethical, immoral or abusive conduct rather than simple ineffective teaching). However, benign behavior is not teaching—it is more often maintenance of the status quo. And to those who teach seriously, simply maintenance is not enough. *Power of Teaching* is offered to support the work by identifying behaviors that are least helpful and those that are most helpful—and developing ways to maximize the most helpful.

To collect data meant to provide teachers with feedback using *Power of Teaching* or any other behavior-analysis system, it is critical to consciously heighten awareness of the biases and prejudices that educators—like all mortals—bring to their adult lives. Often biases, like prejudices, are unwitting or even subconscious in nature. Arising from personal experiences, they are often formed as a way to cope with a reality that is often bewildering and occasionally overwhelming; they help us "compartmentalize" and organize. But they can interfere with effective teaching if we don't acknowledge their influence over our interactions with students. Being thoughtful about this human factor simply means we need to remain mindful of each teacher's paradigms or mental filters—things that reveal a predisposition to prejudice and bias that we all have in varying degrees.

Behavioral scientists have repeatedly found that we mentally "filter" what we see, hear, taste, touch and smell through our past experiences and the memories of those past experiences. Because of this human propensity to "filter" what our senses tell us—rather than simply accept objectively what we are sensing—it is important that we at least explore with teacher candidates their experiences—and their values and beliefs relating to the way children learn. Frankly, those who at their core do not believe that all kids can learn and study at high levels ought not to be teachers of anyone's children in the first place. And, for those who observe teaching practices and collect data relating to the effectiveness of those practices, we have to ensure maximum objectivity in the observations. When using *Power of Teaching* effectively one has to be highly conscious of one's own paradigms—which include multiple biases and prejudices.

Seven guiding principles for the use of collecting data on *Power of Teaching* data collection instruments:

1. A minimum of 25 uninterrupted minutes observing teaching behavior to ensure full coverage of the sources of power being observed.
2. Do not use periods of testing or other student assessment activities as a time to collect *Power of Teaching* data. (Testing and assessment sessions are important components of teaching and learning, but are not appropriate activities for *Power of Teaching* observations—

164

except under those limited circumstances when teachers are utilizing test data as part of Power Source 6.0—*Aligning Classroom with the Macro-Organization* in Indicator 6.3—*Strategic Use of Relevant Student Performance Data*

3. Teaching behavior should be coded (tallied) in "real time" as it is observed. No coding should take place outside of the actual observation of a behavior.
4. Code only what is seen or heard.
5. Make vertical tally marks in bundled of fives—on the right-side for effective (more *causal*) behaviors and on the left-side for unhelpful or ineffective behaviors.
6. Do not interact with the teacher or students during the data collection.
7. Collect data during the observation; don't evaluate or draw conclusions.

With respect to Guiding Principle 5, *Power of Teaching* is a different type of classroom observation protocol than in other protocols such as "walk-throughs." Protocols such as walk-throughs, typically involve interaction with students, student testimony, and contemplation of teacher efficacy on the basis of student feedback. To ensure accuracy in *Power of Teaching* observations, it is strongly recommended that in any classroom visit, no disruption of classroom momentum occur. That means simply stepping in discretely, being seated, observing, and collecting data.

Objectivity is of paramount importance when collecting classroom teaching behavioral data. Separating the collection of data from making judgments or drawing conclusions on the data is critical. It is equally essential that *Power of Teaching* be used in a formative, diagnostic, and progress-monitoring manner—not in an evaluative manner. When the Greensboro, North Carolina-based Center for Creative Leadership (CCL) developed its own system of feedback tools for leaders and managers in the early 1990s, CCL stressed that if a change (improvement) is desired, productive, constructive feedback must be applied, accepted, and acted upon. To achieve maximum application, acceptance, and action the feedback must be delivered and contained in truly psychologically-safe scenarios. It cannot stress enough: Even the toughest and most seemingly resilient teachers can be rendered fragile when it comes to criticizing their teaching practices and behaviors. To remain a client and constituent of *Power of Teaching*, this rule is inviolate: the process *must* be executed in a psychologically safe/non-threatening manner. After all, the purpose of *Power of Teaching* is to *enhance* teaching effectiveness—not to undermine teacher self-belief.

165

Giving & Receiving Feedback

The success of an organization is directly proportional to the ability of the team members of that organization to effectively give and receive feedback.
—Jim Huge

For certain, giving and receiving feedback effectively is of paramount importance in implementation of *Power of Teaching*. Effectively giving and receiving feedback is a 2-way process and requires adequate skill and care. Guiding Principles for effectively giving and receiving feedback include the following:

Giving Feedback

As leaders, especially as instructional leaders, it is incumbent upon each of us to master the art of giving performance feedback carefully and in ways that are psychologically safe to those receiving the feedback. Some important critical success factors include the following:

1. Give information that is clear and direct
2. Continue to remind the teacher of his/her efficacy ratios in *Power of Teaching* and reminding him/her of the ongoing to improve their personal best

3. Offer suggestions that are specific and in accordance with the research behind *Power of Teaching*,
4. Answer questions the feedback receiver has, or agree to follow-up once you have an answer.
5. Maintain the teacher's personal and professional dignity and self-esteem at all times during the process of giving feedback
   a. Some teachers prefer to be praised only in private.
   b. Most teachers prefer to receive feedback for improvement *ONLY* in private.
   c. The only permissions granted to use *Power of Teaching* are as a developmental tool—not an evaluative or firing tool!
   d. Truth about a teacher's practice must prevail at all costs.
   e. Be open to the teacher creating greater context for behaviors observed.

Receiving Feedback

As leaders, whether holding positional power (the boss) or referent power (by way of respect garnered solely through one's leadership works and deeds) we owe it to our teacher colleagues to help them master the art of receiving feedback effectively. Important and critical success factors include the following:

1. Asking for the information and for clarifying information
2. Listening intently to complete messages provided by the feedback giver
3. Asking clarifying questions to ensure understanding
4. Requesting information or resources to solve problems
5. Accepting suggestions for improvement and growth

Ginger Hopkins suggests that we must honor teachers by:
1. Scheduling sufficient time with and for the teacher with
2. Dialogue- asking what they noted were relative strengths and weaknesses by always
3. Discussing next steps.

As we are reminded of the most powerful element of leadership: modeling, we must remember to also model these critical success factors when *we* receive feedback from our teachers and other colleagues. Modeling is one of the most powerful teaching practices, especially for adults.

Teamwork

In the end, systematizing *Power of Teaching* requires teamwork. Teamwork between the instructional leaders and the teachers. Mike Walls reminded me of the mantra of Frank Broyles, former head coach of the University of Arkansas football team: "The best players don't always make up the best teams; but the best teams always win." Transfer that to a school's faculty and think of that faculty as a team. Teamwork is always required to win. Winning for children is the mantra to which we must subscribe.

If more emphasis on teamwork is needed, remind school colleagues of Marty Schotenheimer, former NFL football coach whose leadership taught us, *"Individuals win games but teams win championships."*

Notes:

167

Notes

Chapter Twelve
What's Next

Powering-up a teacher's teaching practice is all about a continuous journey of self evaluation, reflection and deliberation for teachers and their coaches and leaders. It is not a destination, nor is there a "silver bullet" that somehow instantly achieves teaching perfection. *Power of Teaching* was designed to help us—as individual instructional leaders and teachers—develop a heightened awareness of *how* our behaviors (often innocuous and unintended) influence the way our students learn. By focusing on the way we communicate with students, and on the way we structure each lesson and classroom activity, it *is* possible to make lasting, and sustainable, differences in student academic growth. And, it's not rocket science. Instead, use of *Power of Teaching can be* a common sense approach to teaching effectiveness that arises from decades of education research and "best practices" analysis— and lays out each critical factor in each Power Source.

Atlantic Research Partners has launched a 5-year Teaching Efficacy Project focused on raising student achievement through teachers themselves. This project is designed to accomplish the following critical milestones in the coming months:

1. Further the research behind each of the 44 effective teaching Indicators comprising *Power of Teaching*.
2. Codify and disseminate the best-practices among our client partners in *Power of Teaching* Power Source 6.0—*Aligned Expectations to Macro-Organization*, and customize for subscribing clients each of the key components of *Power of Teaching*.
3. The convening of groups of educators—who seek to develop or enhance their instructional leadership acumen—and provide them with access to best practices training and development.
4. Research and identify additional effective teaching behaviors that are more *causal* (and not simply correlative to) student learning.
5. Team with highly qualified experts as co-authors to expand the foundational research for *Power of Teaching* into specific subject/con-tent and practice areas:
   a. *Power of Teaching* in early grade Reading and Writing
   b. *Power of Teaching* in Mathematics
   c. *Power of Teaching* in the Visual & Performing Arts

d. ***Power of Teaching*** in the Social Studies
e. ***Power of Teaching*** in the Sciences, Engineering and Technology fields
f. ***Power of Teaching*** in Special Education

Atlantic Research Partners, is an organization committed to two core goals: (1) Accelerating and sustaining academic improvements in America's educational systems and (2) Strengthening leadership efficacy for America's businesses, institutions, and service agencies.

If you desire more information about *Atlantic Research Partners*, please visit the website URL:

www.atlanticresearchpartners.org

To order additional copies of ***Power of Teaching***-- *the Science of the* Art please call Victor Frush, Director of Publications, 904-322-1276. You may also order books by emailing bookorders@atlanticresearchpartners.org

Notes:

Notes:

170

APPENDIX 1

Focusing & Engaging Minds

Inter-Rater Mastery

Observed Teacher Behavior

1. Teacher analyzed and presented material which led to students' acquisition of concepts

Indicator 2.2	**Effective**	**Right-side tally**

   or

Indicator 3.4	**Effective**	**Right-side tally**

2. Teacher provided the meaning of a key term during the lesson without an example or further analysis.

Indicator 2.6	**Ineffective**	**Left-side tally**

3. Teacher directed students in using a principle or law to solve a problem.

Indicator 3.4	**Effective**	**Right-side tally**

4. Teacher specified an action, event, or object that stimulated students to evaluate the presented material.

Indicator 2.5	**Effective**	**Right-side tally**

5. Teacher attended to a task and extinguished a disruption at the same time, and kept the lesson going all at the same time.

Indicator 3.5	**Effective**	**Right-side tally**

   or

Indicator 4.6	**Effective**	**Right-side tally**

6. Teacher kept students, as a group, focused on the work of reciting answers to her review questions

Indicator 3.6a	**Effective**	**Right-side tally**

172

7. Teacher avoided an abrupt stop and kept the lesson moving

    Indicator 3.5   **Effective**   **Right-side tally**

8. Teacher provided several situations to help students apply the academic concept.

    Indicator 3.4   **Effective**   **Right-side tally**

9. Teacher behavior indicated he was angry

    Indicator 1.3   **Ineffective**   **Left-side tally**

10. Teacher statement demonstrated empathy and amplified positive relationship to students.

    Indicator 1.1   **Effective**   **Right-side tally**

11. Teacher engaged in multiple actions or talk beyond what was necessary for students to understand or learn how to participate in the group activity or use of classroom equipment.

    Indicator 2.3   **Ineffective**   **Left-side tally**
          or
    Indicator 3.5   **Ineffective**   **Left-side tally**

12. Teacher behavior emphasized attributes that separated a family of concepts (e.g. executive branch, judicial branch, legislative branch) and encouraged students to reflect on the distinct attributes.

    Indicator 2.5   **Effective**   **Right-side tally**

13. Teacher explained circumstances to which an academic concept applies.

    Indicator 2.6   **Effective**   **Right-side tally**

14. Teacher directed students in determining that the correct rule was applied and solutions were properly reached.

    Indicator 2.6   **Effective**   **Right-side tally**

APPENDIX 2

Focusing & Engaging Minds
Managing Learners for Learning

Observation Instruments

SOURCE	INEFFECTIVE	Tally	Sum	Sum	Tally	EFFECTIVE
1.0 Cognitive Connections for Learning (& Teaching)	1.1 Negative Reinforcing Verbals/Nonverbals					1.1 Effective Verbals/Nonverbals
	1.2 Ineffective Grammar/Diction					1.2 Effective Grammar/Diction
	1.3 Questioning with Insufficient Wait Time					1.3 Questioning/Sufficient wait time
	1.4 Harsh/No Redirection to Incorrect Responses					1.4 Effectively Guided Incorrect Answers
	1.5 Indifferent Engagement of Students					1.5 Application with Real-World Relevance
	1.6 Use of General Praise					1.6 Applied Specific Academic Praise
	1.0 Total/Ratio	%			%	**1.0 Ratio/Total**
2.0 Pacing & Productivity for Learning	2.1 Missed Opportunity to Adjust Pacing When Needed					2.1 Use of Differentiated Pacing
	2.2 Introduced New Concept/Activity or No Comprehension Check					2.2 Checked for Academic Understanding
	2.3 Extended Discourse					2.3 Specific Dialogue to Excite Learning
	2.4 Unproductive Remediation or *Busy Work*					2.4 Applied Grade Level Rigor
	2.5 Indifferent Engagement of Students					2.5 Engagement w/ Real-World Rigor
	2.6 Use of Standalone Discourse					2.6 Effectively Applied Academic Rule w/Examples
	2.0 Total/Ratio	%			%	**2.0 Ratio/Total**
3.0 Transitions, Processes & Endings for Learning	3.1 Ineffective/Unclear Transitions					3.1 Made Lesson Transitions Explicit/Clear
	3.2 Irrelevant Opening Activity					3.2 Opened the Lesson/Topic with Clarity
	3.3 Downtime/Wasted Minutes					3.3 *Bell-to-Bell* Instruction
	3.4 Moved to New Concept w/No Practice					3.4 Provided for Relevant Academic Practice
	3.5 Allowed/Created Fragmentation or Unproductive Discourse					3.5 Maintained Academic Flow/Pacing
	3.6 Irrelevant/Overuse of Recall Questioning					3.6a Differentiated/Strategic Use of Questioning
						3.6b Strategic Use of Higher Order Questioning — 3.6b1 Required Student Analysis of Topic
						3.6b2 Required Student Academic Reasoning on Topic
						3.6b3 Required Student Synthesis on Topic
						3.6b4 Required Student Academic Judgment of Topic
	3.0 Total/Ratio	%			%	**3.0 Ratio/Total**

Atlantic Research Partners   *Power of Teaching*   Managing Learners for Learning

Teacher _____   Date _____   Time _____   Subj/Grade _____

SOURCE	INEFFECTIVE	Tally	Sum	Sum	Sum	Tally	EFFECTIVE
4.0 On-Task Learning	4.1 Circulated with no Explicit Purpose-or Remained at Desk						4.1 Circulated & Assisted w/Instructional Purpose
	4.2 Group Chastisement/Consequences						4.2 Redirection/Disciplined in Private
	4.3 Academic Concepts without Examples/Non-examples (Standalone Discourse)						4.3 Made Student-centered Meaning w/ Examples or Non-Examples
	4.4 Counting/Sorting Materials on the Fly						4.4 Advanced Sorting of Materials
	4.5 Use of General Praise						4.5 Applied Specific Academic Praise
	4.6 Delays Behavior Management						4.6 Stopped Misconduct Strategically
	4.0 Total/Ratio	%				%	**4.0 Ratio/ Total**
5.0 Differentiated Teaching to Accelerate Learning	5.1 Missed Opportunity for Activity Grouping or Grouping with no Strategic Intent Apparent						**5.1 Flexible Grouping for Accelerating Learning** — 5.1a Flexible/Groups for Accelerating Learning
							5.1b Strategic use of Heterogeneous Grouping
							5.1c Strategic use of Homogenous Grouping
	5.2 Under-utilized Classroom Furniture						5.2 Strategic Use of Furniture to Flexibly Group
	5.3 Under-utilized adult(s) to enable learning						5.3 Strategic Use of Adult(s) to Flexibly Group
	5.4 Under-utilized achievement/Activity Data						5.4 Strategic Use of Data to Flexibly Group
	5.5 Ignored Student Engagement/Responses						5.5 Accentuated Academic Responses with Linking Words
	5.6 Missed Opportunity for Emphasis or Amplifying						5.6 Emphasized Salient Academic Points
	5.0 Total/Ratio	%				%	**5.0 Ratio/Total**
6.0 Aligned Expectations to Macro-Organization	6.1 Unrelated *Busy-work Materials* in Use						6.1 Approved Materials in Full Use
	6.2 Non/Misused/Under-Resourced Walls						6.2 Teacher Arranged Artifacts In-Use
	6.3 Non/Ineffective-Use of Student Performance Data						6.3 Strategic Use of Relevant Student Performance Data
	6.4 No Student Work Posted						6.4 Teacher Arranged/Displayed Student Work
	6.5 Non/Misuse of Word-Walls						6.5 Grade-level Endorsed use of Word-Walls
	6.6						6.6
	6.7						6.7
	6.8						6.8
	6.0 Total/Ratio	%				%	**6.0 Ratio/Total**

Teacher _____   Date _____   Time _____   Subj/Grade _____

SOURCE	INEFFECTIVE	Tally	Sum	Sum	Tally	EFFECTIVE
1.0 Cognitive Connections for Learning (& Teaching)	1.1 Negative Reinforcing Verbals/Nonverbals					1.1 Effective Verbals/Nonverbals
	1.2 Ineffective Grammar/Diction					1.2 Effective Grammar/Diction
	1.3 Questioning with Insufficient Wait Time					1.3 Questioning/Sufficient wait time
	1.4 Harsh/No Redirection to Incorrect Responses					1.4 Effectively Guided Incorrect Answers
	1.5 Indifferent Engagement of Students					1.5 Application with Real-World Relevance
	1.6 Use of General Praise					1.6 Applied Specific Academic Praise
	1.0 Total/Ratio	%			%	**1.0 Ratio/Total**
2.0 Pacing & Productivity for Learning	2.1 Missed Opportunity to Adjust Pacing When Needed					2.1 Use of Differentiated Pacing
	2.2 Introduced New Concept/Activity or No Comprehension Check					2.2 Checked for Academic Understanding
	2.3 Extended Discourse					2.3 Specific Dialogue to Excite Learning
	2.4 Unproductive Remediation or *Busy Work*					2.4 Applied Grade Level Rigor
	2.5 Indifferent Engagement of Students					2.5 Engagement w/ Real-World Rigor
	2.6 Use of Standalone Discourse					2.6 Effectively Applied Academic Rule w/Examples
	2.0 Total/Ratio	%			%	**2.0 Ratio/Total**
3.0 Transitions, Processes & Endings for Learning	3.1 Ineffective/Unclear Transitions					3.1 Made Lesson Transitions Explicit/Clear
	3.2 Irrelevant Opening Activity					3.2 Opened the Lesson/Topic with Clarity
	3.3 Downtime/Wasted Minutes					3.3 *Bell-to-Bell* Instruction
	3.4 Moved to New Concept w/No Practice					3.4 Provided for Relevant Academic Practice
	3.5 Allowed/Created Fragmentation or Unproductive Discourse					3.5 Maintained Academic Flow/Pacing
	3.6 Irrelevant/Overuse of Recall Questioning					3.6a Differentiated/Strategic Use of Questioning
						3.6b Strategic Use of Higher Order Questioning
						3.6b1 Required Student Analysis of Topic
						3.6b2 Required Student Academic Reasoning on Topic
						3.6b3 Required Student Synthesis on Topic
						3.6b4 Required Student Academic Judgment of Topic
	3.0 Total/Ratio	%			%	**3.0 Ratio/Total**

Atlantic Research Partners *Power of Teaching* Managing Learners for Learning

Power of Teaching, second edition. Copyright © 2010 by Atlantic Research Partners, LLC. Reproduced by permission of Atlantic Research Partners, LLC.

Teacher _____ Date _____ Time _____ Subj/Grade _____

SOURCE	INEFFECTIVE	Tally	Sum	Sum	Tally	EFFECTIVE
4.0 On-Task Learning	4.1 Circulated with no Explicit Purpose-or Remained at Desk					4.1 Circulated & Assisted w/Instructional Purpose
	4.2 Group Chastisement/Consequences					4.2 Redirection/Disciplined in Private
	4.3 Academic Concepts without Examples/Non-examples (Standalone Discourse)					4.3 Made Student-centered Meaning w/ Examples or Non-Examples
	4.4 Counting/Sorting Materials on the Fly					4.4 Advanced Sorting of Materials
	4.5 Use of General Praise					4.5 Applied Specific Academic Praise
	4.6 Delays Behavior Management					4.6 Stopped Misconduct Strategically
	4.0 Total/Ratio	%			%	**4.0 Ratio/ Total**
5.0 Differentiated Teaching to Accelerate Learning	5.1 Missed Opportunity for Activity Grouping or Grouping with no Strategic Intent Apparent					5.1 Flexible Grouping for Accelerating Learning: 5.1a Flexible/Groups for Accelerating Learning; 5.1b Strategic use of Heterogeneous Grouping; 5.1c Strategic use of Homogenous Grouping
	5.2 Under-utilized Classroom Furniture					5.2 Strategic Use of Furniture to Flexibly Group
	5.3 Under-utilized adult(s) to enable learning					5.3 Strategic Use of Adult(s) to Flexibly Group
	5.4 Under-utilized achievement/Activity Data					5.4 Strategic Use of Data to Flexibly Group
	5.5 Ignored Student Engagement/Responses					5.5 Accentuated Academic Responses with Linking Words
	5.6 Missed Opportunity for Emphasis or Amplifying					5.6 Emphasized Salient Academic Points
	5.0 Total/Ratio	%			%	**5.0 Ratio/Total**
6.0 Aligned Expectations to Macro-Organization	6.1 Unrelated *Busy-work Materials* in Use					6.1 Approved Materials in Full Use
	6.2 Non/Misused/Under-Resourced Walls					6.2 Teacher Arranged Artifacts In-Use
	6.3 Non/Ineffective-Use of Student Performance Data					6.3 Strategic Use of Relevant Student Performance Data
	6.4 No Student Work Posted					6.4 Teacher Arranged/Displayed Student Work
	6.5 Non/Misuse of Word-Walls					6.5 Grade-level Endorsed use of Word-Walls
	6.6					6.6
	6.7					6.7
	6.8					6.8
	6.0 Total/Ratio	%			%	**6.0 Ratio/Total**

Teacher _____ Date _____ Time _____ Subj/Grade _____

Atlantic Research Partners   *Power of Teaching*   Focusing & Engaging Minds

Power of Teaching, second edition. Copyright © 2010 by Atlantic Research Partners, LLC. Reproduced by permission of Atlantic Research Partners, LLC.

SOURCE	INEFFECTIVE	Tally	Sum	Sum	Tally	EFFECTIVE
1.0 Cognitive Connections for Learning (& Teaching)	1.1 Negative Reinforcing Verbals/Nonverbals					1.1 Effective Verbals/Nonverbals
	1.2 Ineffective Grammar/Diction					1.2 Effective Grammar/Diction
	1.3 Questioning with Insufficient Wait Time					1.3 Questioning/Sufficient wait time
	1.4 Harsh/No Redirection to Incorrect Responses					1.4 Effectively Guided Incorrect Answers
	1.5 Indifferent Engagement of Students					1.5 Application with Real-World Relevance
	1.6 Use of General Praise					1.6 Applied Specific Academic Praise
	1.0 Total/Ratio	%			%	**1.0 Ratio/Total**
2.0 Pacing & Productivity for Learning	2.1 Missed Opportunity to Adjust Pacing When Needed					2.1 Use of Differentiated Pacing
	2.2 Introduced New Concept/Activity or No Comprehension Check					2.2 Checked for Academic Understanding
	2.3 Extended Discourse					2.3 Specific Dialogue to Excite Learning
	2.4 Unproductive Remediation or *Busy Work*					2.4 Applied Grade Level Rigor
	2.5 Indifferent Engagement of Students					2.5 Engagement w/ Real-World Rigor
	2.6 Use of Standalone Discourse					2.6 Effectively Applied Academic Rule w/Examples
	2.0 Total/Ratio	%			%	**2.0 Ratio/Total**
3.0 Transitions, Processes & Endings for Learning	3.1 Ineffective/Unclear Transitions					3.1 Made Lesson Transitions Explicit/Clear
	3.2 Irrelevant Opening Activity					3.2 Opened the Lesson/Topic with Clarity
	3.3 Downtime/Wasted Minutes					3.3 *Bell-to-Bell* Instruction
	3.4 Moved to New Concept w/No Practice					3.4 Provided for Relevant Academic Practice
	3.5 Allowed/Created Fragmentation or Unproductive Discourse					3.5 Maintained Academic Flow/Pacing
	3.6 Irrelevant/Overuse of Recall Questioning					3.6a Differentiated/Strategic Use of Questioning
						3.6b Strategic Use of Higher Order Questioning — 3.6b1 Required Student Analysis of Topic
						3.6b2 Required Student Academic Reasoning on Topic
						3.6b3 Required Student Synthesis on Topic
						3.6b4 Required Student Academic Judgment of Topic
	3.0 Total/Ratio	%			%	**3.0 Ratio/Total**

Atlantic Research Partners   *Power of Teaching*   Managing Learners for Learning

Teacher _____   Date _____   Time _____   Subj/Grade _____

SOURCE	INEFFECTIVE	Tally	Sum	Sum	Tally	EFFECTIVE
4.0 On-Task Learning	4.1 Circulated with no Explicit Purpose–or Remained at Desk					4.1 Circulated & Assisted w/Instructional Purpose
	4.2 Group Chastisement/Consequences					4.2 Redirection/Disciplined in Private
	4.3 Academic Concepts without Examples/Non-examples (Standalone Discourse)					4.3 Made Student-centered Meaning w/ Examples or Non-Examples
	4.4 Counting/Sorting Materials on the Fly					4.4 Advanced Sorting of Materials
	4.5 Use of General Praise					4.5 Applied Specific Academic Praise
	4.6 Delays Behavior Management					4.6 Stopped Misconduct Strategically
	4.0 Total/Ratio	%			%	**4.0 Ratio/ Total**
5.0 Differentiated Teaching to Accelerate Learning	5.1 Missed Opportunity for Activity Grouping or Grouping with no Strategic Intent Apparent					5.1 Flexible Grouping for Accelerating Learning — 5.1a Flexible/Groups for Accelerating Learning / 5.1b Strategic use of Heterogeneous Grouping / 5.1c Strategic use of Homogenous Grouping
	5.2 Under-utilized Classroom Furniture					5.2 Strategic Use of Furniture to Flexibly Group
	5.3 Under-utilized adult(s) to enable learning					5.3 Strategic Use of Adult(s) to Flexibly Group
	5.4 Under-utilized achievement/Activity Data					5.4 Strategic Use of Data to Flexibly Group
	5.5 Ignored Student Engagement/Responses					5.5 Accentuated Academic Responses with Linking Words
	5.6 Missed Opportunity for Emphasis or Amplifying					5.6 Emphasized Salient Academic Points
	5.0 Total/Ratio	%			%	**5.0 Ratio/Total**
6.0 Aligned Expectations to Macro-Organization	6.1 Unrelated *Busy-work Materials* in Use					6.1 Approved Materials in Full Use
	6.2 Non/Misused/Under-Resourced Walls					6.2 Teacher Arranged Artifacts In-Use
	6.3 Non/Ineffective-Use of Student Performance Data					6.3 Strategic Use of Relevant Student Performance Data
	6.4 No Student Work Posted					6.4 Teacher Arranged/Displayed Student Work
	6.5 Non/Misuse of Word-Walls					6.5 Grade-level Endorsed use of Word-Walls
	6.6					6.6
	6.7					6.7
	6.8					6.8
	6.0 Total/Ratio	%			%	**6.0 Ratio/Total**

Teacher _____   Date _____   Time _____   Subj/Grade _____

Atlantic Research Partners *Power of Teaching* Focusing & Engaging Minds

Power of Teaching, second edition. Copyright © 2010 by Atlantic Research Partners, LLC. Reproduced by permission of Atlantic Research Partners, LLC.

SOURCE	INEFFECTIVE	Tally	Sum	Sum	Tally	EFFECTIVE
1.0 Cognitive Connections for Learning (& Teaching)	1.1 Negative Reinforcing Verbals/Nonverbals					1.1 Effective Verbals/Nonverbals
	1.2 Ineffective Grammar/Diction					1.2 Effective Grammar/Diction
	1.3 Questioning with Insufficient Wait Time					1.3 Questioning/Sufficient wait time
	1.4 Harsh/No Redirection to Incorrect Responses					1.4 Effectively Guided Incorrect Answers
	1.5 Indifferent Engagement of Students					1.5 Application with Real-World Relevance
	1.6 Use of General Praise					1.6 Applied Specific Academic Praise
	1.0 Total/Ratio	%			%	**1.0 Ratio/Total**
2.0 Pacing & Productivity for Learning	2.1 Missed Opportunity to Adjust Pacing When Needed					2.1 Use of Differentiated Pacing
	2.2 Introduced New Concept/Activity or No Comprehension Check					2.2 Checked for Academic Understanding
	2.3 Extended Discourse					2.3 Specific Dialogue to Excite Learning
	2.4 Unproductive Remediation or *Busy Work*					2.4 Applied Grade Level Rigor
	2.5 Indifferent Engagement of Students					2.5 Engagement w/ Real-World Rigor
	2.6 Use of Standalone Discourse					2.6 Effectively Applied Academic Rule w/Examples
	2.0 Total/Ratio	%			%	**2.0 Ratio/Total**
3.0 Transitions, Processes & Endings for Learning	3.1 Ineffective/Unclear Transitions					3.1 Made Lesson Transitions Explicit/Clear
	3.2 Irrelevant Opening Activity					3.2 Opened the Lesson/Topic with Clarity
	3.3 Downtime/Wasted Minutes					3.3 *Bell-to-Bell* Instruction
	3.4 Moved to New Concept w/No Practice					3.4 Provided for Relevant Academic Practice
	3.5 Allowed/Created Fragmentation or Unproductive Discourse					3.5 Maintained Academic Flow/Pacing
	3.6 Irrelevant/Overuse of Recall Questioning					3.6a Differentiated/Strategic Use of Questioning
						3.6b Strategic Use of Higher Order Questioning — 3.6b1 Required Student Analysis of Topic
						3.6b2 Required Student Academic Reasoning on Topic
						3.6b3 Required Student Synthesis on Topic
						3.6b4 Required Student Academic Judgment of Topic
	3.0 Total/Ratio	%			%	**3.0 Ratio/Total**

Teacher _____ Date _____ Time _____ Subj/Grade _____

SOURCE	INEFFECTIVE	Tally	Sum	Sum	Tally	EFFECTIVE
4.0 On-Task Learning	4.1 Circulated with no Explicit Purpose-or Remained at Desk					4.1 Circulated & Assisted w/Instructional Purpose
	4.2 Group Chastisement/Consequences					4.2 Redirection/Disciplined in Private
	4.3 Academic Concepts without Examples/Non-examples (Standalone Discourse)					4.3 Made Student-centered Meaning w/ Examples or Non-Examples
	4.4 Counting/Sorting Materials on the Fly					4.4 Advanced Sorting of Materials
	4.5 Use of General Praise					4.5 Applied Specific Academic Praise
	4.6 Delays Behavior Management					4.6 Stopped Misconduct Strategically
	4.0 Total/Ratio	%			%	**4.0 Ratio/ Total**
5.0 Differentiated Teaching to Accelerate Learning	5.1 Missed Opportunity for Activity Grouping or Grouping with no Strategic Intent Apparent					5.1 Flexible Grouping for Accelerating Learning — 5.1a Flexible/Groups for Accelerating Learning
						5.1b Strategic use of Heterogeneous Grouping
						5.1c Strategic use of Homogenous Grouping
	5.2 Under-utilized Classroom Furniture					5.2 Strategic Use of Furniture to Flexibly Group
	5.3 Under-utilized adult(s) to enable learning					5.3 Strategic Use of Adult(s) to Flexibly Group
	5.4 Under-utilized achievement/Activity Data					5.4 Strategic Use of Data to Flexibly Group
	5.5 Ignored Student Engagement/Responses					5.5 Accentuated Academic Responses with Linking Words
	5.6 Missed Opportunity for Emphasis or Amplifying					5.6 Emphasized Salient Academic Points
	5.0 Total/Ratio	%			%	**5.0 Ratio/Total**
6.0 Aligned Expectations to Macro-Organization	6.1 Unrelated *Busy-work Materials* in Use					6.1 Approved Materials in Full Use
	6.2 Non/Misused/Under-Resourced Walls					6.2 Teacher Arranged Artifacts In-Use
	6.3 Non/Ineffective-Use of Student Performance Data					6.3 Strategic Use of Relevant Student Performance Data
	6.4 No Student Work Posted					6.4 Teacher Arranged/Displayed Student Work
	6.5 Non/Misuse of Word-Walls					6.5 Grade-level Endorsed use of Word-Walls
	6.6					6.6
	6.7					6.7
	6.8					6.8
	6.0 Total/Ratio	%			%	**6.0 Ratio/Total**

Teacher _____ Date _____ Time _____ Subj/Grade _____

Atlantic Research Partners — *Power of Teaching* — Focusing & Engaging Minds

SOURCE	INEFFECTIVE	Tally	Sum	Sum	Tally	EFFECTIVE
1.0 Cognitive Connections for Learning (& Teaching)	1.1 Negative Reinforcing Verbals/Nonverbals					1.1 Effective Verbals/Nonverbals
	1.2 Ineffective Grammar/Diction					1.2 Effective Grammar/Diction
	1.3 Questioning with Insufficient Wait Time					1.3 Questioning/Sufficient wait time
	1.4 Harsh/No Redirection to Incorrect Responses					1.4 Effectively Guided Incorrect Answers
	1.5 Indifferent Engagement of Students					1.5 Application with Real-World Relevance
	1.6 Use of General Praise					1.6 Applied Specific Academic Praise
	1.0 Total/Ratio	%			%	**1.0 Ratio/Total**
2.0 Pacing & Productivity for Learning	2.1 Missed Opportunity to Adjust Pacing When Needed					2.1 Use of Differentiated Pacing
	2.2 Introduced New Concept/Activity or No Comprehension Check					2.2 Checked for Academic Understanding
	2.3 Extended Discourse					2.3 Specific Dialogue to Excite Learning
	2.4 Unproductive Remediation or *Busy Work*					2.4 Applied Grade Level Rigor
	2.5 Indifferent Engagement of Students					2.5 Engagement w/ Real-World Rigor
	2.6 Use of Standalone Discourse					2.6 Effectively Applied Academic Rule w/Examples
	2.0 Total/Ratio	%			%	**2.0 Ratio/Total**
3.0 Transitions, Processes & Endings for Learning	3.1 Ineffective/Unclear Transitions					3.1 Made Lesson Transitions Explicit/Clear
	3.2 Irrelevant Opening Activity					3.2 Opened the Lesson/Topic with Clarity
	3.3 Downtime/Wasted Minutes					3.3 *Bell-to-Bell* Instruction
	3.4 Moved to New Concept w/No Practice					3.4 Provided for Relevant Academic Practice
	3.5 Allowed/Created Fragmentation or Unproductive Discourse					3.5 Maintained Academic Flow/Pacing
	3.6 Irrelevant/Overuse of Recall Questioning					3.6a Differentiated/Strategic Use of Questioning
						3.6b Strategic Use of Higher Order Questioning
						3.6b1 Required Student Analysis of Topic
						3.6b2 Required Student Academic Reasoning on Topic
						3.6b3 Required Student Synthesis on Topic
						3.6b4 Required Student Academic Judgment of Topic
	3.0 Total/Ratio	%			%	**3.0 Ratio/Total**

Atlantic Research Partners   *Power of Teaching*   Managing Learners for Learning

Teacher_____ Date_____ Time_____ Subj/Grade_____

SOURCE	INEFFECTIVE	Tally	Sum	Sum	Tally	EFFECTIVE
4.0 On-Task Learning	4.1 Circulated with no Explicit Purpose-or Remained at Desk					4.1 Circulated & Assisted w/Instructional Purpose
	4.2 Group Chastisement/Consequences					4.2 Redirection/Disciplined in Private
	4.3 Academic Concepts without Examples/Non-examples (Standalone Discourse)					4.3 Made Student-centered Meaning w/ Examples or Non-Examples
	4.4 Counting/Sorting Materials on the Fly					4.4 Advanced Sorting of Materials
	4.5 Use of General Praise					4.5 Applied Specific Academic Praise
	4.6 Delays Behavior Management					4.6 Stopped Misconduct Strategically
	4.0 Total/Ratio	%			%	**4.0 Ratio/ Total**
5.0 Differentiated Teaching to Accelerate Learning	5.1 Missed Opportunity for Activity Grouping or Grouping with no Strategic Intent Apparent					5.1a Flexible/Groups for Accelerating Learning / 5.1b Strategic use of Heterogeneous Grouping / 5.1c Strategic use of Homogenous Grouping / 5.1 Flexible Grouping for Accelerating Learning
	5.2 Under-utilized Classroom Furniture					5.2 Strategic Use of Furniture to Flexibly Group
	5.3 Under-utilized adult(s) to enable learning					5.3 Strategic Use of Adult(s) to Flexibly Group
	5.4 Under-utilized achievement/Activity Data					5.4 Strategic Use of Data to Flexibly Group
	5.5 Ignored Student Engagement/Responses					5.5 Accentuated Academic Responses with Linking Words
	5.6 Missed Opportunity for Emphasis or Amplifying					5.6 Emphasized Salient Academic Points
	5.0 Total/Ratio	%			%	**5.0 Ratio/Total**
6.0 Aligned Expectations to Macro-Organization	6.1 Unrelated *Busy-work Materials* in Use					6.1 Approved Materials in Full Use
	6.2 Non/Misused/Under-Resourced Walls					6.2 Teacher Arranged Artifacts In-Use
	6.3 Non/Ineffective-Use of Student Performance Data					6.3 Strategic Use of Relevant Student Performance Data
	6.4 No Student Work Posted					6.4 Teacher Arranged/Displayed Student Work
	6.5 Non/Misuse of Word-Walls					6.5 Grade-level Endorsed use of Word-Walls
	6.6					6.6
	6.7					6.7
	6.8					6.8
	6.0 Total/Ratio	%			%	**6.0 Ratio/Total**

Teacher_____ Date_____ Time_____ Subj/Grade_____

Index

186

References

Advani, K. and Beaumaster, E. (1973). The rise of behavior modification techniques in a class of slow learners. Kingston, Ontario: Frontenac County Board of Education.

Abraham, E., Nelson, M., and Reynolds, W. (1971). Discussion strategies and student cognitive skills. A paper presented at the annual meeting of the American Educational Research Association, New York.

Addington, D. (1971). The effect of vocal variations on ratings of source credibility. Speech Monographs, 38: 242-247.

Adler, S. (2009). "Three Views from the Corner Office". Businessweek.

Allen, E. (1981). A study of the relationship between teacher enthusiasm and selected student variables in area vocational schools. Dissertation Abstracts International, 42(3): 1114A.

Allington, R. (1980). Teacher interruption behaviors during primary-grade oral reading. Journal of Educational Psychology, 371-377.

Anastasi, A. and Cordova, F. (1953). Some effects of bilingualism upon the intelligence test performance of Puerto Rican children in New York City. Journal of Educational Psychology, 44: 1-19.

Anderson, L., Evertson, C., and Brophy, J. (1978). The first grade reading group study: Technical report of experimental effects and process-outcome relationships. Elementary School Journal 79/4 (March 1979): 193-223.

Anderson, L., Evertson, C., and Emmer, E. (1980). Dimensions in classroom management derived from recent research. Journal of Curriculum Studies, 12: 343-356.

Anderson, L. and Evertson, C. (1978). Classroom organization at the beginning of school: Two case studies. Paper presented to the American Association of colleges for Teacher Education, Chicago.

Anderson, L., Brubaker, N., Alleman-Brooks, J., Duffy, G. (1985). A qualitative study of seatwork in first-grade classrooms. The Elementary School Journal, 86(2): 123-140.

Andrews, G. and Debus, R. (1978). Persistence and casual attribution of failure. Modifying cognitive attributions. Journal of Educational Psychology, 70: 154-166.

Antion, D. and Michael, W. (1983). Short-term predictive validity of demographic, affective, personal, and cognitive variables in relation to two criterion measures of cheating behaviors. Educational and Psychological Measurement, 43: 467-482.

Arlin, M. (1979). Teacher transitions can disrupt time flow in classroom. American Educational Research Journal, 16.

Austin, J. (1974). Homework research in mathematics 1900-1974. Paper presented at the 1974 Annual Georgia Mathematics Education Conference, Rock Eagle, GA.

Austin, J. (1976). Do comments on mathematics homework affect student achievement? School Science and Mathematics, 76: 159-164.

Ausubel, D. (1960). The use of advance organizers in the learning and retention of meaningful material. Journal of Educational Psychology, 51: 267-272.

Ausubel, D., and Youssef, M. (1965). The effect of spaced repetition on meaningful retention. Journal of General Psychology, 73: 147-150.

Bangert-Drowns, R., Kulik, J., and Kulick, C. (1983). Effects of coaching programs on achievement test performance. Review of Educational Research, 53(4): 571-585.

Barger, G. W. (1983). Classroom testing procedures and student anxiety. Improving College and University Teaching, 31(1): 25-26.

Barker, G. and Graham, S. (1987). Developmental study of praise and blame as attributional cues. Journal of Educational Psychology, 79(1): 62-66.

Barringer, C. and Gholson, B. (1979). Effects of type and combination of feedback upon conceptual learning by children: Implications for research in academic learning. Review of Educational Research, 49: 459-478.

Bates, J. (1979). Extrinsic reward and intrinsic motivation: A review with implications for the classroom. Review of Educational Research, 49: 557-576.

Bauer, D. (1975). The effects of instructions, anxiety and locus of control on intelligence test scores. Measurement and Evaluation in Guidance, 8: 12-19.

Beasley, W. (1983). Teacher management behaviors and pupil task involvement during small group laboratory activities. Journal of Research in Science Teaching. 20(8): 713-719.

Becker, W. (1988). Direct Instruction: Special issue. Education and Treatment of Children, 11: 297-402.

Becker, W., et al. (1968). Production and elimination of disruptive classroom behavior by systematically varying teacher's behavior. Journal of Applied Behavior Analysis, 1: 35-45.

Bellack, A. et al. (1966). The Language of the Classroom. New York: Teachers College Press.

Bemis, K. and Luft, M. (1970). Relationships between teacher behavior, pupil behavior, and pupil achievement. In Simon and Beyer (Eds.) Mirrors for Behavior: An Anthology of Observation Instruments Continued, Supplement, Vol. A Philadelphia, PA: Research for Better Schools.

Bennett, S. (1978). Recent research on teaching: A dream, a belief, and a model. British Journal of Educational Psychology, 48: 127-147.

192

Ben-Peretz, M. and Kremer-Hayon, L. (1990). The content and context of professional dilemmas encountered by novice and senior teachers. Educational Review, 42(1): 31-40.

Benson, J., Urman, H. and Hocevar, D. (1986). Effects of test-wiseness training and ethnicity on achievement of third- and fifth-grade students. Measurement and Evaluation in Counseling and Development, 18(4): 154-162.

Berliner, D.. (1982). Recognizing instructional variables. Introduction to Education, edited by D.E. Orlosky. Columbus, Ohio: Charles E. Merrill, 198-225.

Berliner, D. (1988). The development of expertise in pedagogy. Charles W. Hunt Memorial Lecture presented to the American Association of Colleges for Teacher Education, New Orleans.

Berliner, D.. (1988). Implications of studies of expertise in pedagogy for teacher education and evaluation. Paper presented at the Educational Testing Service Conference on new Directions for Teacher Assessment, New York.

Bettencourt, E. (1979). Effects of training teachers in enthusiasm on student achievement and attitudes. Dissertation Abstracts International, 40: 3237A.

Blanck, P., et al. (1970). The effect of verbal reinforcement on intrinsic motivation for sex-linked tasks. Paper presented at the annual meeting of the American Psychological Association.

Bligh, H. (1965). Trends in the measurement of educational achievement. Review of Educational Research, 35: 34-49.

Bloom, B. (1976). Human characteristics and school learning. New York: McGraw-Hill.

Borg, W. (1969). The minicourse as a vehicle for changing behavior: The research evidence. Far West Laboratory for Educational Research and Development.

Borg, W. (1975). Protocol Materials as related to teacher performance and pupil achievement. Journal of Educational Research, 69: 23-30.

Borg, W. (1980). Time and school learning. In C. Denham and A. Liberman (Eds.) Time to Learn. Washington, D.C.: The National Institute of Education, U.S. Department of Education.

Borg, W. and Ascione, F. (1982). Classroom management in elementary mainstreaming classrooms. Journal of Educational Psychology, 74: 85-95.

Borg, W. et al., (1975). Teacher classroom management skills and pupil behavior. Journal of Experimental Education, 44: 52-58.

193

Borich, G. and Fenton, K. (1977). The Appraisal of Teaching: Concepts and process. Reading, MA: Addison and Wesley.

Borko, H. and Livingston, C. (1989). Cognition and Improvisation: Differences in mathematics instruction by expert and novice teachers. American Educational Research Journal, 26(4): 473-498.

Brackbill, Y. and Kappy, M. (1962). Delay of reinforcement and retention. Journal of Comparative and Physiological Psychology, 55: 14-18.

Brandt, R. (1998). Powerful learning. Alexandria, VA: American Association for Supervision & Curriculum Development.

Bridgeman, B. (1974). Effects of test score feedback on immediately subsequent test performance. Journal of Educational Psychology, 66: 62-66.

Brophy, J. (1979). Teacher behavior and student learning. Educational Leadership, 37: 33-38.

Brophy, J. (1981). Teacher praise: a functional analysis. Review of Educational Research, 51: 5-32.

Brophy, J. and Evertson, C. (1974). Process-Product Correlations in the Texas Teacher Effectiveness Study: Final Report. Austin: University of Texas at Austin.

Brophy, J. and Evertson, C. (1974). Presentation of non-linear relationships and summary discussion. The Texas Teacher Effectiveness Project, Report No. 74-6. Austin: University of Texas Center for Teacher Education.

Brophy, J. and Evertson, C. (1976). Learning from Teaching: A Developmental Perspective. Boston: Allyn and Bacon.

Brophy, J. and Good, T. (1970). Teacher's communication of differential expectations for children's classroom performance: Some behavioral data. Journal of Educational Psychology, 61: 365-374.

Brophy, J. (1996). Teaching problem students. New York: Guilford.

Brophy, J. and Putman, J. (1978). Classroom Management in the elementary grades. East Lansing, Michigan: Institute for Research on Teaching, Michigan State University.

Brown, D. (1988). Twelve middle-school teachers' planning. The Elementary School Journal, 89(1): 69-87.ol teachers' planning. The Elementary School Journal, 89(1): 69-87.

Buckley, P.and Cooper, J. (1978). An ethnography study of an elementary school teacher's establishment and maintenance of group norms. Paper presented to the American Educational Research Association, Toronto.

Bullough, R. Jr. (1987). Planning and the first year of teaching. Journal of Education for Teaching, 13(3): 231-250.

Burgoon, J. (1979). Attributes of the newscaster's voice as predictors of his credibility. Journal quarterly, 55: 276-281.

Burr, W. (1963). Empirical relationships among modes of testing, modes of instruction and reading levels: In sixth grade social studies. Journal of Experimental Education, 31: 433-435.

Bushway, A. and Nash, W. (1977). School cheating behavior. Review of Educational Research, 147: 623-632.

Butler, R. and Nisan, M. (1986). Effects of no feedback, task-related comments, and grades on intrinsic motivation and performance. Journal of Educational Psychology. 78(3): 210-216.

Cain, B. (1989). With world making planning models matter. English Education, 21(1): 5-29.

Calkins, L. (2001). The art of teaching reading. New York: Addison-Wesley.

Calkins, L. (1994). The art of teaching writing. Toronto: Irwin.

Cameron, L. and Heywood, J. (Spring 1985). Better testing: give them the questions first. College Teaching, 34: 76-77.

Campbell, J. (1973). Pattern analysis – a macroscopic development for interaction analysis. Paper presented at the National Association for Research in Science Teaching, annual Meeting, Chicago.

Carrier, C. and Titus, A. (1981). Effects of notetaking, pretraining and text mode expectations on learning from lecture. American Educational Research Journal, 18: 385-397.

Carroll, J. B. (1963). A model for school learning. Teacher's College Record, 64: 723-733.

Carter, J. and Lee, A. (1989). Preactive planning and conceptions of success in elementary health education. Journal of School Health, 59(1): 13-17.

Carter, K; Cushing, K; Sabers, D.; Stein, P. and Berliner, D. (1988). Expert novice differences in perceiving and processing visual classroom information. Journal of Teacher Education, 39(3): 25-31.

Carter, L. (2009). Five big ideas leading total instructional alignment. Bloomington, IN: Solution Tree.

Carver, R. (1973). Effect of increasing the rate of speech presentation upon comprehension. Journal of Educational Psychology, 65: 118-126.

Chabot, A. (1984). Elementary teachers' perceptions of curriculum work: A descriptive study using self-report data and teachers' view on selected variables. Doctoral dissertation, The University of Connecticut, Dissertation Abstracts International, 46: 596.

Chaiken, A., Sigler, E., & Derlega, V. (1974). Nonverbal mediators of teacher expectancy effects. Journal of Personality and Social Psychology, 30(1): 144-149.

Chapin, M. and Dyck, D. (1975). Persistence in children's reading behavior as a function of N length and attrition retaining. Journal of Abnormal Psychology, 85: 511-515.

Clark, C. (1978). A new question for research on teaching. Educational Research Quarterly, 3: 53-58.

Clark, C. and Elmore, J. (1979). Teacher planning in the first weeks of school. Research Series, No. 56. East Lansing: Michigan State University, Institute for Research on Teaching.

Clawson, T., Firment, C., and Trower, T. (1981). Test anxiety: Another origin for racial bias in standardized testing. Measurement and Evaluation in Guidance, 13: 210-215.

Coats, W. and Smidchens, U. (1966). Audience recall as a function of speaker dynamism. Journal of Educational Psychology, 57: 189-191.

Coker, H., Lorentz, J., and Coker, J. (1976). Interim Report on County CBTC Project, Fall, 1976. Atlanta: Georgia State Department of Education.

Collins, M. (1978). Effects of enthusiasm training on preservice elementary teachers. Journal of Experimental Psychology, 103(2): 263-268.

Cooke, D. and Brown, G., Jr. (1935). Home study has many angles. Journal of Education, 118: 409-410.

Cooper, H. and Baron, R. (1977). Academic expectations and attributed responsibility as predictors of teacher's reinforcement behavior. Journal of Educational Psychology, 69: 409-418.

Cooper, H. and others (1979). Gender differences in the academic locus of control beliefs of young children (Research Report). Center for the Study of Social Behavior, University of Missouri, Columbia.

Copeland, W. (1987). Classroom management and student teachers' cognitive abilities: A relationship. American Educational Research Journal, 24(2): 219-236.

Cotler, S. and Palmer, R. (1970). The effects of test anxiety, sex of subject, and type of verbal reinforcement on maze performance of elementary school children. Journal of Personality, 38: 216-234.

Covington, M. and Omelich, C. (1987). I knew it cold before the exam: A test of the anxiety-blockage hypothesis. Journal of Educational Psychology, 79(4): 393-400.

Crawford, C., and Carmichael, J. (1937). The value of home study. Elementary School Journal, 38: 194-200.

Crawford, W., King, C., Brophy, J., and Evertson, C. (1975). Error rates and question difficulty related to elementary children's learning. Paper presented at the American Educational Research Association, Washington, D.C.

Crocker, L. and Schmidt, A. (1987). Improving multiple-choice test performance for examinees with different levels of test anxiety. Journal of Experimental Education, 55: 201-205.

Crocker, R. and Brooker, G. (1986). Classroom control and student outcomes in grades 2 and 5. American Educational Research Journal. 23(1): 1-11.

Cubberly, W., Weinstein, C., and Cubberly, R. (January 1986). The interactive effects of cognitive learning strategy training and test anxiety on paired-associate learning. Journal of Educational Psychology, 72: 16-20.

Curtis, H. and Kropp, R. (1961). A comparison of scores obtained by administering a test normally and visually. Journal of Experimental Education. 29: 249-260.

Dalton, W. (1969). The relationships between classroom interactions and teacher ratings of pupils: An exploration of one means by which a teacher may communicate her expectations. Peabody Papers in Human Development, 7: 6.

Danielson, C. (1998). Teaching for Mastery, Practitioner's Implementation Handbook, Eye on Education, INC.

Darch, C. and Gersten, R. (1985). The effects of teacher presentation rate and praise on LD students' oral Reading Performance. British Journal of Educational Psychology, 55: 295-303.

Deaton, W. Halpin, G., and Alford, T. (January 1987). Coaching effects on California Achievement Test scores in elementary grades. Journal of Educational Research, 80(3): 149-155.

Denham, C. and Lieberman, A. (1980). Time to Learn. Washington, D.C.: National Institute of Education.

Di Napoli, P. (1937). Homework in the new york city schools. New York: Columbia Teachers College.

Diehl, C. and McDonald, E. (1956). Effect of voice quality on communication. Journal of Speech and Hearing Disorders, 21: 233-237.

Diehl, C., White, R. and Satz, P. (1961). Pitch change and comprehension. Speech Monographs, 28: 65-68.

Dillon, J. (1982). The multidisciplinary study of questioning. Journal of Educational Psychology, 74: 147-164.

Dolly, J. and Williams, K. (1986). Using test-taking strategies to maximize multiple-choice test scores. Educational and Psychological Measurement, 46: 619-624.

Doyle, W. (1984). How order is achieved in classrooms: An interim report. Journal of Curriculum Studies, 16(3): 259-277.

Doyle, W. (1984). How order of expectations and attributions in the alleviation of learned helplessness. Journal of Personality and Social Psychology, 31: 674-685.

Dreisbach, M. and Keogh, B. (1982). Testwiseness as a factor in readiness test performance of young Mexican-American children. Journal of Educational Psychology, 74: 224-229.

197

Duchastel, P. and Merrill, P. (1973). The effects of behavioral objectives on learning. A review of empirical studies. Review of Educational Research, 43: 53-69.

Dunkin, M. and Biddle, B. (1974). The Study of Teaching. New York: Holt, Rinehart and Winston.

Duschl, R. and Wright, E. (1989). A case study of high school teachers' decision making models for planning and teaching science. Journal of Research in Science Teaching, 26(6): 467-501.

Dweck, C. et al. (1978). Sex differences in learned helplessness: II. The contingencies of evaluative feedback in the classroom and III. An experimental analysis. Developmental Psychology, 14: 268-276.

Edmunds, R. (1979). Effective schools for the urban poor. Educational Leadership, 37: 15-18, 20-24.

Ehrensberger, R. (1945). An experimental study of the relation effectiveness of certain forms of emphasis in public speaking. Speech Monographs, 12: 94-111.

Ehrenworth, M. & Vinton, V. (2005). The power of grammar. Portsmouth, NH: Heineman.

Eisner, E. (1967). Educational objectives: Help or hindrance? School Review, 75:250-66.

Elawar, M. and Corno, L. (1985). A factorial experiment in teachers' written feedback on student homework: changing teacher behavior a little rather than a lot. Journal of Educational Psychology, 77(2): 162-173.

Emmer, E., Evertson, C. and Brophy, J. (1979). Stability of teacher effects in junior high classrooms. American Educational Research Journal, 16: 71-75.

Emmer, E., Evertson, C. and Anderson, L. (1980). Effective classroom management at the beginning of the school year. Elementary School Journal, 80: 219-231.

Evans, E. and Craig, D. (1990). Teacher and student perceptions of academic cheating in middle and senior high schools. Journal of Educational Research, 84(1): 44-52.

Evans, R. Venetozzi, R., Bundrick, M., and McWilliams, E. (1988). The effects of sentence-combining instructions on writing and on standardized test scores. Journal of Educational Research, 82(1): 53-56.

Evans, W. and Guymon, R. (1978). Clarity of explanation: A powerful indicator of teacher effectiveness. Paper presented at meeting of the American Educational Research Association, Toronto.

Evertson, C. (1980). Differences in instructional activities in high and low achieving junior high classes. Paper presented at the annual meeting of the American Educational Research Association, Boston.

198

Evertson, C., Anderson, C., Anderson, L., and Brophy, J. (1980). Relationships between classroom behaviors and student outcomes in junior high mathematics and English classes. American Educational Research Journal, 17: 43-60.

Evertson, C. (1989). Improving elementary classroom management: A school-based training program for beginning the year. Journal of Educational Research, 83(2): 82-90.

Evertson, C. and Weade, R. (1989). Classroom management and teaching styles: Instructional stability and variability in two junior high English classrooms. The Elementary School Journal, 89(3): 379-393.

Evertson, C.; Emmer, E.; Sanford, J. and Clements, B. (1983). Improving classroom management: An experiment in elementary school classrooms. The Elementary School Journal, 84(2): 173-189.

Fagan, E., Hassler, D. and Szabo, M. (1981). Evaluation of questioning strategies in language arts instruction. Research in the Teaching of English, 15(3): 267-273.

Fischer, C. (1970). Levels of cheating under conditions of informative appeal to honest, public affirmation of value and threats of punishment. Journal of Educational Research, 64: 12-16.

Fisher, C., Berliner, D., Filby, N., Marliave, R., Cahen, L., and Dishaw, M. (1980). Teaching behaviors, academic learning time, and student achievement: An overview. In C. Denham and A. Lieberman (Eds.) Time to Learn. Washington, D.C.: The National Institute of Education, U.S. Department of Education.

Fisher, C.W., Filby, N., Marliave, R., Cahen, L., Dishaw, M., Moore, J., and Berliner, D. (1978). Technical Report V-1: Teaching behaviors, academic learning time and student achievement: Final report of phase III-B, Beginning Teacher Evaluation Study. San Francisco: Far West Laboratory.

Flanders, N. (1970). Analyzing teacher behavior. Reading, PA: Addison Wesley.

Floden, R.: Porter, A. Schmidt, W.; Freeman, D. and Schwille, J. (1981). Responses to curriculum pressures: A policy-capturing study of teacher decisions about content. Journal of Educational Psychology, 73(2): 129-141.

FPMS—Florida Performance Measurement (1989). Unspecified Authors. State of Florida Department of Education. Tallahassee: Unpublished manuscripts.

Fountas, I. & Pinnell, G. (2001). Guiding readers and writers. Portsmouth, NH: Heineman.

Frederick, W. (1977). The use of classroom time in high schools above or below the median reading score. Urban Education, 459-464.

199

French, J. (1962). Effect of anxiety on verbal and mathematical examination scores. Educational and Psychology Measurement, 22: 553-564.

Fry, B. (1984). A descriptive study of elementary teachers' instructional planning. Doctoral dissertation, University of South Florida, Dissertation Abstracts International, 46: 339.

Fryer, R. (2006). Acting White. Education Next. New York, NY.

Fuchs, D. and Fuchs, L. (1986). Test procedure bias: A meta-analysis of examiner familiarity effects. Review of Educational Research, 56(2): 243-262.

Gall, M. (1970). The use of questions in teaching. Review of Educational Research, 40: 707-721.

Ganz, B. and Ganz, M. (1988). Overcoming the problem of learned helplessness. College Teaching, 36(2): 82-84.

Gay, L. (1973). Temporal position of reviews and its effect on the retention of mathematical rules. Journal of Educational Psychology, 64: 171-182.

Gazzaniga, M. (2008). Human. New York: HarperCollins, 367.

Gillett, M. (1980). Effects of teacher enthusiasm on at-risk behavior of students in elementary classes. Dissertation Abstracts International, 41(5): 1919A.

Glover, J. (1989). The "testing" phenomenon: Not gone but nearly forgotten. Journal of Educational Psychology, 81(3): 392-399.

Glutting, J. and McDermott, P. (1989). Using "teaching items" on ability tests: A nice idea but does it work? Educational and Psychological Measurement, 49: 257-268.

Glynn, E. et al. (1973). Behavioral self-control of on-task behavior in an elementary classroom. Journal of Applied Behavioral Analysis, 6: 105-113.

Golden, N., Gersten, R., and Woodward, J. (1990). Effectiveness of guided practice during remedial reading instruction: an application of computer-managed instruction. The Elementary School Journal, 90(3): 291-304.

Goldstein, A. (1960). Does homework help? A review of research. Elementary School Journal, 1: 212-224.

Good, T. and Beckerman, T. (1978). The effect of classroom context on student achievement. Technical Report No. 145. Center for Research in Social Behavior, University of Missouri, Columbia.

Good, T. and Beckerman, T. (1978). Time on task: A naturalistic study in sixth grade classrooms. Elementary School Journal, 73: 193-201.

Good, T. and Brophy, J. (1979). Looking in Classrooms. (9th edition). Boston: Allyn & Bacon.

Good, T. and Grouws, D. (1975). Process-product relationship in fourth grade mathematics classrooms. Columbia: University of Missouri.

Good, T. and Grouws, D. (1977). Teachers manual: Missouri mathematics effectiveness project. Columbia, MO: Center for Research in Social Behavior, University of Missouri.

Good, T. and Grouws, D. (1979). The Missouri mathematics effectiveness project: An experimental study in fourth grade classrooms. Journal of Educational Psychology, 71: 339-362.

Good, T., and Biddle, B., and Brophy, J. (1975). Teachers make a difference. New York: Holt, Rinehart, and Winston.

Goodlad, J., Klein, M., et al. (1974). Looking behind the classroom door. Worthington, OH: Charles A. Jones Publishing.

Gorden, L. and Durea, M. (1948). The effect of discouragement on the revised Stanford-Binet scale. Journal of Genetic Psychology, 73: 201-207.

Gray, R. and Allison, D. (1971). An experimental study of the relationship of homework to pupil success in computation with fractions. Social Science and Mathematics, 71: 339-346.

Green, K. (1981). Item-response changes on multiple-choice tests as a function of test anxiety. Journal of Experimental Education, 49: 225-228.

Greenwood, C., et al. (1974). Group contingencies for group consequences in classroom management: A further analysis. Journal of Applied Behavioral Analysis, 7: 413-425.

Gump, P. (1974). Operating environments in schools of open or traditional design. School Review, 82: 575-594.

Gunderson, D. and Hopper, R. (1976). Relationship between speech delivery and speech effectiveness. Communication Monographs, 43: 158-165.

Guthrie, J.., Samuels, S., Marzuta, V., Seifert, M., Tyler, S., and Edwall, G. (1976). A study of the locus and nature of reading problems in the elementary school: Final Report, Section II. Newark, DE: International Reading Association.

Hall, T. (2002). Differentiated instruction. Wakefield, MA: National Center on Accessing the General Curriculum. Retrieved from http://www.cast.org/publications/ncac/ncac_diffinstruc.html

Harris, A. and Serwer, B. (1966). Comparison of reading approaches in first grade teaching with Disadvantaged Children (The Craft Project). New York: Division of Teacher Education, The City of New York.

Harris, A. and Serwer, B. (1966). Instructional time in reading research. The CRAFT project: Reading Research Quarterly, 2: 27-56.

Harris, A., Morrison, C., Serwer, B., and Gold, L. (1968). A Continuation of the CRAFT Project – Comparing Approaches with Disadvantaged Negro Children in Primary Grades. New York: Division of Teacher Education, The City University of New York.

Hawkins, J. and Blakeslee, S. (2004) On intelligence. New York: Henry Holt.

201

Hawkins, J., Doueck, H. and Lishner, D. (1988). Changing teaching practices in mainstream classrooms to improve bonding and behavior of low achievers. American Educational Research Journal. 25(1): 31-50.

Heines, B. and Hawthorne, R. (1978). Sibling-related teacher expectancies and their possible influence on classroom behaviors and achievement levels in seventh grade English classes. Paper presented at annual meeting of American Educational Research Association.

Hembree, R. (1988). Correlates, causes, effects and treatment of test anxiety. Review of Educational Research, 58(1): 47-77.

Herbert, J. and McNergney, R. (1988). Teachers' planning for and implementation of evaluation in elementary and secondary classrooms. Journal of Research and Development in Education, 22(1): 39-45.

Herman, S. and Traymontana, J. (1971). Instructions and group versus individual reinforcement in modifying disruptive group behavior. Journal of Applied Behavior Analysis, 4: 113-119.

Hill, J.; Yinger, R. and Robins, D. (1983). Instructional planning in a laboratory preschool. The Elementary School Journal, 83(3): 182-193.

Hiller, J. (1971). Verbal response Indicators of conceptual vagueness. American Educational Research Journal, 8: 151-162.

Hiller, J. et al. (1969). A computer investigation of verbal characteristics of effective classroom lecturing. American Educational Research Journal, 6: 661-675.

Hines, C. (September, 1981). A further investigation of teacher clarity: The relationship between observed and perceived clarity and student achievement and satisfaction. Doctoral Dissertation, Ohio State University.

Hines, C., Cruickshank, D. and Kennedy, J. (1985). Teacher clarity and its relationship to student achievement and satisfaction. American Educational Research Journal, 22(1): 87-99.

Hoffman, J., Clements, R. (1984). Reading miscues and teacher verbal feedback. The Elementary School Journal, 84(4): 423-439.

Hoffman, J., O'Neal, S., Kastler, L., Clements, R., Segel, K., and Nash, M. (1984). Guided oral reading and miscue focused verbal feedback in second-grade classrooms. Reading Research Quarterly, 19(3): 367-384.

Housner, L. and Griffey, D. (1985). Teacher cognition: Differences in planning and interactive decision making between experiences and inexperienced teachers. Research Quarterly for Exercise and Sport, 56(1): 45-53.

Hovland, C. (1938). Experimental studies in Rote-Learning Theory: III. Distribution of practice with varying speech of syllable presentation. Journal of Experimental Psychology, 23: 172-190.

Howell, W. (1982). The empathic communicator. University of Minnesota: Wadsworth Publishing.

202

Hughes, D. (1973). An experimental investigation of the effects of pupil responding and teacher reacting on pupil achievement. American Educational Research Journal, 10: 21-38.

Hunter, M. (1984). Knowing, teaching, and supervising. (Hosford Edition) Using what we know about teaching. (pp. 167-193). Alexandria: Association for Supervision and Curriculum Development.

Ingle, B. and DeAmico, G. (1969). Effect of physical conditions of the test room on standardized achievement test scores. Journal of Educational Measurement, 6: 237-240.

Isacowitz, R. (2006). Successful cuing in pilates. Champagne, IL: Human Kinetics.

Jenkins, O. (2006). From (1995) Techniques: principles and approaches of language learning. Inservice for language teachers at Rosslyn Academy, Nairobi, Kenya.

Jenson, A. (1974). The effect of race of examiner on the mental test scores of white and black pupils. Journal of Educational Measurement, 11: 1-14.

Jersild, A. (1928). Modes of emphasis in public Speaking. Journal of Applied Psychology, 12: 611-620.

Johnson, R. and Klores, M. (1968). Attitudes toward cheating as a function of classroom dissatisfaction and peer norms. Journal of Educational Research, 62: 60-64.

Joyce, B., and Harootunian, B. (1964). Teaching as problem solving. Journal of Teacher Education, 15: 420-427.

Joyce, B. and Weil, M. (1986). Models of teaching. Englewood Cliffs, NJ. Prentice-Hall.

Kalechstein, P., Kalechstein, M., and Doctor, R. (1981). The effects of instruction on test-taking skills in second grade Black children. Measurement and Evaluation in Guidance, 13: 198-202.

Kalish, R. (1958). An experimental evaluation of the open book examination. Journal of Educational Psychology, 49: 200-204.

Kallison, J., Jr. (1986). Effects of lesson organization on achievement. American Educational Research Journal, 23(2): 337-347.

Karweit, N. and Slavin, R. (1982). Time on task: Issues of timing, sampling and definition. Journal of Educational Psychology, 74: 844-851.

Keith, L., Tornatzky, L. and Pettigrew, L. (1974). An analysis of verbal and nonverbal classroom teaching behavior. Journal of Experimental Education, 42: 30-38.

Kennedy, J. et al. (1979). Additional investigations into the nature of teacher clarity. Journal of Educational Research, 72: 3-9.

Kennedy, J., Cruickshank, D., Bush, A. and Myers, B. (1979). Additional investigations into the nature of teacher clarity. Journal of Educational Research, 72: 3-10.

Keppel, G. (1964). Facilitation in short- and long-term retention of paired associates following distributed practice in learning. Journal of Verbal Learning, 3: 91-111.

Kirkland, K. and Hollandsworth, J., Jr. (1979). Test anxiety, study skills, and academic performance. Journal of College Student Personnel, 20: 431-436.

Kirkland, M. (1971). The effect of tests on students and schools. Review of Educational Research, 41: 303-351.

Klein, A. (2009). Interview with Arne Duncan for article: We must do better. Education Week: Washington, DC.

Koch, E., Jr. (1975). Homework in arithmetic. The Arithmetic Teacher, 12: 9-13.

Kohlbert, L. (1969). State and sequence: the cognitive development approach to socialization. In Goslin (Ed.) Handbook of Socialization Theory and Research. Chicago: Rand McNally.

Komulainen, E. and Kansanen, P. (EDS.). (1981). Classroom analysis: Concepts, findings and applications. DPA Helsinki Investigations III, Research Bulletin No. 56. Finland: Helsinki University, Institute of Education, 60 pp.

Kounin, J. (1970). Discipline and group management in classrooms. New York: Holt, Rinehart and Winston.

Kounin, J. and Doyle, P. (1975). Degree of continuity of a lesson's signal system and task involvement of children. Journal of Educational Psychology, 67: 159-164.

Kounin, J. (1983). Classrooms: individual or behavior settings? Micrographs in teaching and learning. (General series No. 1) Bloomington: Indiana University, School of Education. (ERIC Document Reproduction Service No. ED240070).

Kounin, J. et al. (1966). Managing emotionally disturbed children in regular classrooms. Journal of Educational Psychology, 57: 1-13.

Krampen, G. (1987). Differential effects of teacher comments. Journal of Education Psychology, 79(2): 137-146.

Kreutzer, F. (1984). The perceptions of secondary school teachers regarding instructional development. Doctoral dissertation, Columbia University Teachers College, Dissertation Abstracts International, 45.

Kruglanski, A. (1978). Endogenous attribution and intrinsic motivation. In Lepper and Greene (Eds.). The hidden costs of reward: A new perspective on the psychology of human motivation., Hillsdale, NJ: Erlbaum.

Kulik, J. and Kulik, C. (1988). Timing of feedback and verbal learning. Review of Educational Research, 58(1): 79-97.

Kulik, J., Kulik, C., and Bangert, R. (1984). Effects of practice on aptitude and achievement test scores. American Educational Research Journal, 21(2): 435-447.

Lalik, R. and Niles, J. (1990). Collaborative planning by two groups of student teachers. The Elementary School Journal, 90(3): 319-336.

Land, M. and Smith, L. (1979). Effect of a teacher clarity variable on student achievement. Journal of Educational Research, 72: 196-198.

Lee, J., Moreno, K. and Sympson, J. (1986). The effects of mode of test administration on test performance. Educational and Psychological Measurement, 46: 467-473.

Leeper, H. and Thomas, C. (1978). Young children's preferences for listening rates. Perceptual and Motor Skills, 47: 891-898.

Leeper, M. and Dafoe, J. (1979). Incentives, constraints, and motivation in the classroom. In I.H. Frieze and others. New approaches to social problems. San Francisco: Jossey-Bass.

LeGagnoux, G., Michael, W., Hocevar, D., and Macwell, V. (1990). Retest effects on standardized structure-of-intellect ability measures for a sample of elementary school children. Educational and Psychological Measurement, 50: 475-492.

Leinhardt, G. (1983). Overview of a program of research on teachers' and students' routines, thoughts, and execution of plans. Paper presented at the American Educational Research Association, Montreal.

Leinhardt, G., Zigmond, N., and Cooley, W. (1981). Reading instruction and its effects. American Educational Research Journal, 18.

Leonhardt, D. (2009). The big fix. New York: New York *Times,*

Lord, C., Umezaki, K., and Darley, J. (1990). Developmental differences in decoding the meanings of the appraisal actions of teachers. Child Development, 61: 191-200.

Lleras, C. and Rangel, C. (2009). Ability grouping Practices in elementary school and African American /Hispanic achievement. American Journal of Education, 115.

Luiten, J., Ames, W., and Ackerson, G. (1980). Meta-analysis of the effects of advance organizers on learning and retention. American Educational Research Journal, 17: 211-18.

Lysakowski, R. and Walberg, H. (1981). Classroom reinforcement and learning: A quantitative synthesis. Journal of Educational Research, 75: 69-77.

MacDonald, J. (1965). Myths about instruction. Educational Leadership, 22:571-576, 609-617.

Maddox, H. and Hoole, E. (1975). Performance decrement in the lecture. Educational Review, 28: 17-30.

Madsen, C. and Madsen, C. (1998). Teaching/discipline a positive approach for educational development. Chapel Hill: Contemporary Publishing.

Madsen, C. et al. (1968). Rules, praise and ignoring elements of elementary classroom control. Journal of Applied Behavior Analysis, 1: 139-150.

Maehr, M. and Stallings, W. (1972). Freedom from external evaluation, Child Development, 43: 177-185.

Maertens, N. (1969). An analysis of the effects of arithmetic homework upon the arithmetic achievement of third grade pupils. The Arithmetic Teacher, 16: 383-389.

Mager, R. (1962). Preparing Instructional Objectives. Palo Alto, CA: Pearson.

Mahaffey, L., Brophy, J., and Evertson, C. (1975). Teacher feedback to children's answers: process-product relationships. Paper presented to research association, Washington, D.C.

Mann, T. (1975). The practice of planning: The impact of elementary school on teachers' curriculum planning. Doctoral dissertation, University of California, Dissertation Abstracts International, 44.

Manning, B. (1988). Application of cognitive behavior modification: First and third graders' self-management of classroom behaviors. American Educational Research Journal, 25(2): 193-212.

Marsh, J. (1956). Development report: Systematic observation of instructor behavior. San Antonio, TX: Lackland Air Force Base, USAF Personnel Training Research Center.

Marsh, R. (1980). Should we discontinue classroom tests? An experimental study. High School Journal, 63: 288-292.

Marshall, P. (1983). Homework and facilitation theory in teaching elementary mathematics. Unpublished Dissertation, Stanford University.

Martin, J., Veldman, D., and Anderson, L. (1980). Within-class relationships between student achievement and teacher behaviors. American Educational Research Journal, 17: 479-490.

Marzano, R. (2007). The art and science of teaching. Alexandria: Association for Supervision and Curriculum Development.

Marzano, R.., Gaddy, B., Foseid, M., and Marzano, J. (2005). A handbook for classroom management that works. Alexandria: Association for Supervision and Curriculum Development.

Mastin, V. (1963). Teacher enthusiasm. Journal of Educational Research, 56: 385-386.

Mayer, R. (1983). Can you repeat that? Qualitative effects of repetition and advance organizers from science prose. Journal of Educational Psychology, 75: 40-49.

McCarthy, D. (1944). A study of the reliability of the Good Enough Drawing Test of Intelligence. Journal of Psychology, 18: 201-216.

McCoard, C. (1944). Speech factors as related to teaching efficiency. Speech Monographs, 11: 53-64.

McCormick, S. and Hill, D. (1984). An analysis of the effects of two procedures from increasing disabled readers; inferencing skills. Journal of Educational Research, 77(4): 219-226.

McCutcheon, G. (1980). How do elementary school teachers plan their courses? Elementary School Journal, 81:4-23.

McCutcheon, G. (1982). How do elementary school teachers plan? The nature of planning and influences on it. W. Doyle and T. Good (Eds). Focus on Teaching: Readings from the Elementary School Journal. Chicago: University of Chicago Press.

McDonald, F. (1976). Research on teaching and its implications for policy making: Report on Phase II of the Beginning Teacher Evaluation Study. Princeton, NJ: Educational Testing Services.

McDonald, F. and Elias, P. (1976). The effects of teacher performance on pupil learning. Beginning Teacher Evaluation Study, Phase II, Final Report, Vol. I. Princeton, NJ: Educational Testing Service.

McGarity, J., Jr. and Butts, D. (1984). The relationship among teacher classroom management behavior, student engagement and student achievement of middle and high school science students of varying aptitude. Journal of Research in Science Teaching, 21(1): 55-61.

McLaughlin, T. (1976). Self-control in the classroom. Review of Educational Research, 46: 631-663.

McNamera, E., Evans, M. and Hill, W. (1986). The reduction of disruptive behavior in two secondary school classes. British Journal of Educational Psychology, 56: 215-219.

McQueen, R. (1957). Examination deception as a function of residual background and immediate stimulus factors. Journal of Personality, 25: 643-650.

Medley, D. (1977). Teacher competence and teacher effectiveness: A Review of Process-product research. Washington, D.C.: American Association of Colleges for Teacher Education.

Melton, R. (1978). Resolution of conflicting claims concerning the effect of behavioral objectives on student learning. Review of Educational Research, 48: 291-302.

Mendoza, S., Good, T., & Brophy, J. (1972). Who talks in junior high classrooms? Report No. 68. Research and Development center for Teacher Education, University of Texas at Austin.

Merriman, E. (1975). Considerations identified by elementary teachers as elements of their planning for instructional activities. Doctoral dissertation, University of Oregon.

Meyer, W. et al. (1979). The information value of evaluative behavior: influences of praise and blame on perceptions of ability. Journal of Educational Psychology, 71: 259-268.

Mills, S. et al. (1980). The correspondence between teacher questions and student answers in classroom discourse. Journal of Experimental Education, 48: 194-204.

Mims, M. and Gholson, B. (1977). Effects of type and amount of feedback upon hypothesis sampling among 7-8 year old children. Journal of Experimental Child Psychology, 24: 358-371.

Mintz, A. (1979). Teacher planning: A simulation study. Doctoral dissertation, Syracuse University.

Mishra, S. (1980). The influence of examiner's ethnic attributes on intelligence test scores. Psychology in the Schools, 17: 117-122.

Moore, M. (1990). Problem finding and teacher experience. Journal of Creative Behavior, 24(1): 39-58.

Moore, R. and Davies, J. (1984). Predicting GED scores on the bases of expectancy, valence, intelligence, and pretest skill levels with the disadvantaged. Educational and Psychological Measurement, 44: 483-490.

Morine, G. (1976). A study of teacher planning. Special study c (BTES technical report 76-3-1). San Francisco: Far West Laboratory for Educational Research and Development.

Morine-Dershimer, G. (1989). Pre-service teachers' conceptions of content and pedagogy: Measuring growth in reflective, pedagogical decision-making. Journal of Teacher Education, 40(5): 46-52.

Moskowitz, G. and Hayman, J. (1969). Success strategies of inner-city teachers: a year-long study. Journal of Educational Research, 69: 283-89.

Naughton, J. (1968). A modest experiment on test motivation. Personnel and Guidance Journal, 46: 606.

Needels, M. (1988). A new design for process-product research on the quality of discourse in teaching, American Educational Research Journal, 25(4): 503-526.

Neely, A. (1986). Planning and problem solving in teacher education. Journal of Teacher Education, 37(3): 29-33.

Nelson, J., Martell, R., and Galand, B. (1998). The effects of teaching school expectations and establishing a consistent consequence on formal office disciplinary actions. Journal of Emotional and Behavioral Disorders, 4(3) 153-161.

Nichols, J. (1978). The development of the concept of effort and ability, perception of academic attainment and the understanding that difficult tasks require more ability. Child Development, 49: 800-814.

Nichols, J. (1979a). The development of perception of own attainment and causal attributions for success and failure in reading. Journal of Educational Psychology, 71: 94-99.

Nichols, J.G. (1980). Motivational theory and optimum motivation. Paper presented at the annual meeting of the American Educational Research Association.

Nottelman, E. and Hill, K. (1977). Test anxiety and off-task behavior in evaluative situations. Child Development, 48: 225-231.

Ogle, D. (1986). K-W-L: A teaching model that develops active reading of expository text." The Reading Teacher, 39(6), 564-570.

O'Leary, K. and Becker, W. (1968). The effects of a teacher's reprimands on children's behavior. Journal of School Psychology, 7: 8-11.

O'Leary, K., et al. (1970). The effects of loud and soft reprimands on the behavior of disruptive students. Exceptional Children, 37: 145-155.

Oliver, J. and Taylor, B. (1970). The effects of teaching social studies on immediate retention. Journal of Experimental Psychology, 47: 115-121.

Otto, P. and Schuck, R. (1983). The effect of teacher questioning strategy training program on teaching behavior, student achievement, and retention. Journal of Research in Science Teaching, 20(6): 521-528.

Page, E. (1958). Teacher comments and student performance: A seventy-four classroom experiment in school motivation. Journal of Educational Psychology, 49: 173-181.

Pankratz, R. (1967). Verbal interaction patterns in the classroom of selected physics teachers. In Amidon and Hough (Ed.) Interaction Analysis: Theory, Research and Application. Reading: Addison Wesley.

Paulman, R. and Kennelly, K. (1984). Test anxiety and ineffective test taking: Different names, same construct? Journal of Educational Psychology, 76(2): 279-288.

Payne, R. (2008). A framework for understanding poverty. Highlands, TX: Aha! Press.

Payne, B., Smith, J., and Payne, D. (1983). Sex and ethnic differences in relationships of test anxiety to performance in science examinations by fourth and eighth grade students: implications for valid interpretations of achievement test scores. Educational and Psychological Measurement, 43: 267-270.

Peterson, H. et al. (1935). Some measurements of the effects of reviews. Journal of Educational Psychology, 26: 65-72.

Peters, T. (1987). Thriving on chaos: handbook for a management revolution. New York: HarperCollins.

Peterson, P. and Comeaux, M. (1987). Teachers' schemata for classroom events: The mental scaffolding of teachers' thinking during classroom instruction. Teaching and Teacher Education, 3(4): 319-331.

Peterson, P., Marx, R.., and Clark, C. (1978). Teacher planning, teacher behavior and students' achievement. American Educational Research Journal, 15:417-432.

Petrie, C. (1963). Informative speaking: A summary and bibliography of related research. Speech Monographs, 30: 79-91.

Petros, T. and Hoving, K. (1980). The effects if review on young children's memory for prose. Journal of Experimental Child Psychology. 30: 33-43.

Piaget, J. (1951). The child's conception of physical reality. New York: Humanities Press.

Piaget, J. (1970). Piaget's theory. In P. Mussen (Ed.) Carmichael's Manual of Child Psychology, (3rd ed., Vol. 1). New York: Wiley.

Pianta, R. and Allen, J. (2006). What teenagers want. Retrieved from http://news.softpedia.com/news/what-teenagers-want-28627.shtml

Pinney, R. (1969). Presentational behavior related to success in teaching. Doctoral dissertation, Stanford University.

Pittman, T. et al. (1980). Informational vs. controlling rewards, levels of surveillance and intrinsic motivation. Personality and Social Psychology Bulletin, 6: 228-233.

Pompi, K. and Larchman, R. (1967). Surrogate processes in the short-term retention of connected discourse. Journal of Experimental Psychology, 75: 143-150.

Powell, D. and Eash, M. (1974). Secondary school cases. In Walberg, H. (Ed.) Evaluating Educational Performance. Berkeley: McCutchan, 277-293.

Pyle, W. (1913). Economical learning. Journal of Educational Psychology, 4: 148-158.

Rakow, E., Airasian, P. and Madaus, G. (1978). Assessing school and program effectiveness: Estimating teacher level effects. Journal of Educational Measurement, 15: 15-21.

Ratliff, R. (1972). Two-choice discrimination learning in children as a function of punishment modality and reinforcement combination. Journal of Experimental Child Psychology, 14: 365-371.

Redfield, D. and Rousseau, E. (1981). A meta-analysis of research on teacher questioning behavior. Review of Educational Research, 51: 237-245.

Reichenberg-Hackett, W. (1953). Changes in Goodenough drawings after a gratifying . American Journal of Orthopsychiatry, 23: 501-517.

Reynolds, J. and Glasser, R. (1964). Effects of repetition and spaced review upon retention of a complex learning task. Journal of Educational Psychology, 55: 297-308.

Riley, J. II. (1986). The effects of teachers' wait-time and knowledge comprehension questioning on science achievement. Journal of Research in Science Teaching, 23(4): 335-342.

Rim, R. and Collier, A. (1978). In search on non-linear process-product functions in existing schooling-effects data: A reanalysis of the first grade reading and mathematics data from the Stallings and Kaskowitz follow-through study. Philadelphia: Research for Better Schools. (ERIC Document No. ED179289).

Rist, R. (1970). Student social class and teacher expectations: The self-fulfilling prophesy in ghetto education. Harvard Educational Review, 40: 411-451.

Ritter, S. and Idol-Maestas, L. (1986). Teaching middle school students to use a test-taking strategy. Journal of Educational Research, 79(6): 350-357.

Rogosin, H. (1951). What about "cheating" on examinations and honesty? School and Society, 74: 402-403.

Rosenshine, B. (1971). Teaching behaviors and student achievement. London: International Association for the Evaluation of Educational Achievement.

Rosenshine, B. (1976). Recent research on teaching behaviors and student achievement. Journal of Teacher Education, 27: 61-64.

Rosenshine, B. (1978). Academic engaged time, content covered, and direct instruction. Champaign-Urbana: University of Illinois, pp. 37.

Rosenshine, B. (1979). Content, time and direct instruction. In P. Peterson and H. Walberg (Eds.) Research on teaching: Concepts, findings, and implications. Berkeley, CA: McCutchan.

Rosenshine, B. (1980). How time is spent in elementary classrooms. In C. Denham and A. Lieberman (Eds.) Time to Learn. Washington, D.C.: The National Institute of Education, U.S. Department of Education.

Rosenshine, B. (1983). Teaching functions in instructional programs. The Elementary School Journal, 83: 4(335-353).

Rosenthal, R. (1971). Teacher expectation and pupil learning. In R.D. Strom (Ed.) Teachers and the Learning Process. Englewood Cliffs, New Jersey: Prentice-Hall.

Rosswork, S. (1977). Goal setting: The effects on an academic task with varying magnitudes of incentive. Journal of Educational Psychology, 69: 710-715.

Rowe, M. (1974). Wait-time and rewards as instructional variables, their influence on language, logic and fate control: Part on wait-time. Journal of Research in Science Teaching, 11: 81-94.

Rowe, M. (January-February, 1986). Wait-time: Slowing down may be a way of speeding up! Journal of Teacher Education, 43-50.

211

Ruble, D. et al. (1979). Rewards and extrinsic motivation in children: An examination of competence and complexity preference. Paper presented at conference on Teacher and Student Perceptions of Success and Failure and Applications for Learning and Instruction. Pittsburg: University of Pittsburg.

Rubovits, P., and Maehr, M. (1971). Pygmalion analyzed; Toward an explanation of the rosenthal-jacobson findings. Journal of Personality and Social Psychology, 197-2003.

Rutter, M., Maughan, B., Mortimore, P., Ouston, J., with Smith, A. (1979). Fifteen thousand hours. Cambridge, MA: Harvard University Press.

Saigh, P. (1981). The effects of positive examiner verbal comments of the total WISC-R performance of institutionalized EMR students. Journal of School Psychology, 19: 86-91.

Samson, G., Strykowski, B., Weinstein, T. and Walberg, H. (1987). The effects of teacher questioning levels on student achievement: A quantitative synthesis. The Journal of Educational Research, 80(5): 290-295.

Sanford, J. (1984). Management and organization in science classrooms. Journal of Research in Science Teaching, 21(6): 575-587.

Sanford, J. and Evertson, C. (1981). Classroom management in a low SES junior high: three case studies. Journal of Teacher Education, 38: 34-38.

Sanford, J. and Evertson, C. (1983). Time use and activities in junior high classes. Journal of Educational Research, 76(3): 141-147.

Sardo, D. (1986). Instructional decision-making in middle schools. Case studies of teacher planning. Dissertation Abstracts, 47: 3375.

Schoen, H. and Kreye, B. (1974). Five forms of written feedback to homework in a mathematics course for elementary teachers. Journal of Teacher Education, 38-43.

Schuck, R. (1985). An empirical analysis of the power of set induction and systematic questioning as instructional strategies. Journal of Teacher Education, March-April 1985), 38-43.

Schultz, J. and Florio, S. (1979). Stop and freeze: The negotiation of social and physical space in a kindergarten/first grade classroom. Anthropology and Education Quarterly, 10:No. 3.

Schwarz, J. (1967). A new procedure for administering objective tests to large classes. Journal of Educational Measurement, 4: 167-168.

Schwenk, T. and Whitman, N. (1993). Residents as teachers: a guide to educational practice. Salt Lake City: Utah School of Medicine.

Seifert, E. and Beck, J. Jr. (1984). Relationship between task time and leaning gains in secondary schools. Journal of Educational Research, 78(1): 5-9.

Shannon, A. (1980). Effects of methods of standardized reading achievement test administration on attitudes toward reading. Journal of Reading, 23: 684-686.

Shavelson, R. and Stern, P. (1981). Research on teachers' pedagogical thoughts, judgments, decisions and behavior. Review of Educational Research, 51: 455-498.

Shelton, A. (1985). The relative contribution of test information to teachers' educational decisions. Dissertations Abstracts International, 46(5).

Shirk, E. and Hoffman, R. (1961). The academic setting of the dishonest student. Improving College and University Teaching, 9: 130-134.

Shrum, J. (1985). Wait-time and the use of target or native languages. Foreign Language Annals, 18(4): 305-313.

Slakter, M., Koehler, R., and Hampton, S. (1970). Grade level, sex and related aspects of testwiseness. Journal of Educational Measurement, 7: 119-122.

Slotnik, W. et al. (2006) New directions in christina: accomplishments for children, challenges ahead. Boston: Community Training and Assistance Center.

Smith, B. et al. (1962). A Study of the Logic of Teaching. Urbana, IL: University of Illinois Press.

Smith, C. (1969). The origin and expression of achievement-related motives in children. In C.P. Smith (Ed.) Achievement-Related Motives in Children. New York: Russel Sage Foundation.

Smith, L. (1977). Aspects of teacher discourse and student achievement in mathematics. Journal of Research in Mathematics Education, 8: 195-204.

Smith, L. (1984). Effect of teacher vagueness and use of lecture notes on student performance. Journal of Educational Research, 78(2): 69-74.

Smith, L. (1985). Teacher clarifying behaviors: Effects on student achievement and perceptions. Journal of Experimental Education, 53(3): 162-169.

Smith, L. (1985). The effect of lesson structure and cognitive level of questions on student achievement. Journal of Experimental Education, 54(1): 44-49.

Smith, L. and Cotton, M. (1980). Effect of lesson vagueness and discontinuity on student achievement and attitudes. Journal of Educational Psychology, 72: 670-675.

Smith, L. and Edmonds, E. (1978). Teacher vagueness and pupil participation in mathematics learning. Journal for Research in Mathematics Education, 9: 228-232.

Smith, L. and Hedgin, B. (1984-85). A low-inference Indicator of lesson structure in mathematics. Journal of Experimental Education, 53(2): 102-105.

213

Smith, L. and Land, M. (1980). Student perception of teacher clarity in mathematics. Journal of Research in Mathematics Education, 11: 137-146.

Soar, R. (1966). An Integrative Approach to Classroom Learning. Philadelphia: Temple University.

Soar, R. (1968). Optimum teacher-pupil interaction for pupil growth. Educational Leadership Research Supplement, 275-280.

Soar, R. and Soar, R. (1973). Classroom behavior, pupil characteristics and pupil growth for the school year and the summer. Gainesville: University of Florida.

Soar, R. and Soar, R. (1978). Setting variables, classroom interaction and multiple outcomes. Final Report for the National Institute of Education, Project No. 6-0432, Gainesville: University of Florida.

Soar, R. (1973). Follow-through classroom process measurement and pupil growth (1970-1971) (Final Report). Gainesville: University of Florida.

Soars, R. and Soar, R. (1979). Emotional climate and management. In P. Peterson and H. Walberg (Eds.) Research on Teaching. Berkeley: McCutchan Publishing, 97-119.

Solomon, D. and Kendall, A. (1976). Final Report: Individual characteristics and children's performance in varied educational settings. Chicago: Spencer Foundation Project.

Solomon, D., Rosenberg, L. and Bezdek, W. (1964). Teacher behavior and student learning. Journal of Educational Psychology, 55: 23-30.

Spaulding, R. (1965). Achievement creativity and self concepts correlates of teacher-pupil transactions in elementary schools. Cooperative Research Project Report No. 1352. Hempstead, NY: Hofstra University.

Spence, J. (1970). The distraction effects of material reinforcers in the discrimination learning of lower and middle class children. Child Development, 41: 103-111.

Spitzer, H. (1939). Studies in retention. Journal of Educational Psychology, 30: 641-656.

Stallings, J. (1981). Testing teachers' in-class instruction and measuring change resulting from staff development. Paper prepared for National Teacher Examination Policy Council. Princeton, NJ.

Stallings, J. and Kaskowitz, D. (1974). Follow-through classroom observation Evaluation, 1972-73. A Study of Implementation, Menlo Park, CA: Stanford Research Institute, Stanford University.

Stallings, J. and Robertson, A. (1979). Factors influencing women's decisions to enroll in elective mathematics classes in high school. Final Report to the National Institute of Education. Menlo Park, CA: SRI International.

Stallings, J., Needels, M. and Stayrook, N. (1979). How to change the process of teaching basic reading skills in secondary schools. Menlo Park, CA: SRI International.

Stein, P. and Berliner, D. (1988). Expert, novice and postulant teachers' thoughts during teaching. Paper presented at the American Educational Research Association, New Orleans.

Steininger, M., Johnson, R., and Kirts, D. (1964). Cheating on college examinations as a function of situationally aroused anxiety and hostility. Journal of Educational Psychology, 55: 317-324.

Stewart, L. and White, M. (1976). Teacher's comments, letter grades and student performance: what do we really know? Journal of Educational Psychology, 68: 488-500.

Strickland, C. (2004). Leading your school in the implementation of differentiated instruction. In a conference on differentiated instruction for grades preK-12 for Christina School District educators. Wilmington, DE.

Stroot, S. and Morton, P. (1989). Blueprints for learning. Journal of Teaching in Physical Education, 8: 213-222.

Sullivan, H. et al. (1971). Effects of systematic practice on the composition skills of first graders. Elementary English, 51: 635-41.

Super, D., Braasch, W., Jr., and Shay, J. (1947). The effects of distractions on test results. Journal of Educational Psychology, 38: 373-377.

Surber, J. and Anderson, R. (1975). Delay-retention effect in natural classroom settings. Journal of Educational Psychology, 67: 170-173.

Swanson, E. and Deblassie, R. (1979). Interpreter and Spanish administration effects on the WISC performance of Mexican-American children. Journal of School Psychology, 17: 231-236.

Swift, N. and Gooding, C. (1983). Interaction of wait time feedback and questioning instruction on middle school science teaching, Journal of Research in Science Teaching, 20(8): 721-730.

Szafran, R. (1981). Question-pool study guides: Effects on test anxiety and learning retention. Teacher Sociology, 9: 31-43.

Tallal, P. (2008). Interview on how the brain works with interviewer David Boulton. Retrieved from http://www.childrenofthecode.org/interviews/talla.htm

Taylor, M. (1979). Race, sex, and the expression of self-fulfilling prophesies in a laboratory teaching situation. Journal of Personality and Social Psychology. 897-912.

Taylor, P. (1970). How teachers plan their course. Slough, Bucks: National Foundation for Educational Research.

Teahan, G. (1935). Required homework is unwise. The American School Board Journal. 91: 41.

Tenenbaum, G. (1988). The relationship between the quality of instruction and intellectual achievement responsibility following positive and negative educational outcomes. Journal of Experimental Education, 56)32): 1540159.

Tennyson, R., Youngers, J., and Suebsonthi, P. (1983). Concept learning by children using presentation forms for protoptype formation and classification-skill development. Journal of Educational Psychology, 75.

Thompson, E. (1960). An experimental investigation of the relative effectiveness of organizational structure in oral communication. Southern Speech Journal, 26: 59-69.

Tikunoff, W. and Ward, B. (1978). A naturalistic study of the initiation of students into three classroom social systems. San Francisco: Far West Laboratory for Educational Research and Development, Report A-78-11.

Tobin, K. (1984). Effects of extended wait time on discourse characteristics and achievement in middle school grades. Journal of Research in Science Teaching, 21(8): 779-791.

Tobin, K. (1986). Effects of teacher wait time on discourse characteristics in mathematics and language arts classes. American Educational Research Journal, 23(2): 191-200.

Tobin, K. (1987). The role of wait time in higher cognitive level learning. Review of Educational Research, 57(1): 69-95.

Tobin, K. and Capie, W. (1982). Relationships between classroom process variables and middle school science achievement. Journal of Educational Psychology, 74: 441-454.

Tomlinson, C. (2005). How to differentiate instruction in mixed ability classrooms. Alexandria, VA: Association for Supervision and Curriculum Development. (2nd ed.). Upper Saddle River, NJ: Pearson Education.

Traxler, A. and Hilkert, R. (1942). Effect on type of desk on results of machine-scored tests. School and Society, 56: 277-296.

Trentham, L. (1975). The effect of distractions on sixth-grade students in a testing situation. Journal of Educational Measurement, 12: 13-18.

Trentham, L. (1979). Anxiety and instruction effects on sixth-grade students in a testing situation. Psychology in the Schools, 16:439-443.

Uhlig, G.. and Howes, B. (1967). Attitude toward cheating and opportunistic behavior, Journal of Educational Research, 60: 411-412.

Underwood, B. (1961). Ten years of massed practice on distributed practice. Psychological Review, 68: 229-47.

Van Der Ploeg, H. and Hulshof, R. (1984). Cross-cultural study of the relationship among academic performance, test anxiety, intelligence, and sex. Psychological Reports, 55: 343-346.

Vincent, H. (1937). An experiment test of the value of homework in grades 5 and 6. National Elementary Principal, 16: 199-203.

Vitro, F. and Schoer, L. (1972). The effects of probability of test success, test importance, and risk of detection the incidence of cheating. Journal of School Psychology, 10: 269-277.

Wagner, T. (2008). The global achievement gap: why even our best schools don't teach the new survival skills—and what we can do about it. Basic Books: New York.

Walker, R., Sannito, T., and Firetto, A. (1970). The effect of subjectively reported anxiety on intelligence test performance. Psychology in the Schools, 7: 241-243.

Weiner, B. (1979). A theory of motivation for some classroom experiences. Journal of Educational Psychology, 71: 3-25.

Weingarten, R. (2009). A new day for our nation—and our schools. New York *Times.*

Weldon, L. (1966). Cheating in the schools: Teachers are partners in crime. Journal of Educational Research, 19: 19-28.

Wheldall, K., Bevan, K., and Shortall, K. (1986). A touch of reinforcement: The effects of contingent teacher touch on the classroom behavior of young children. Educational Review, 38(3): 207-216.

White, J. (1986). Planning practices of effective high school teachers in a Florida school district. Doctoral dissertation, University of Florida, Dissertation Abstracts, 47(11).

Wiggins, G. and McTighe, J. (1998). Understanding by design. Alexandria, VA: Association for Supervision and Curriculum Development.

Wine, J. (1971). Test anxiety and direction of attention. Psychological Bulletin, 76: 92-104.

Winne, P. (1979). Experiments relating teachers' use of higher cognitive questions to student achievement. Review of Educational Research, 13-50.

Winston, A., et al. (1978). Children's self-reinforcement: Some evidence for maximization of payoff and minimization of effort. Child Development, 49: 882-884.

Wise, K. and Okey, J. (1983). A meta-analysis of the effects of various science teaching strategies on achievement. Journal of Research in Science Teaching, 20(5): 419-435.

Wise, S., Duncan, A., and Plake, B. (1985). The effect of introducing third graders to the use of separate answer sheets on the ITBS. Journal of Educational Research, 78(5): 306-309.

Wright, C. and Nuthall, G. (1970). Relationship between teacher behaviors and pupil achievement in three experimental elementary science lessons. American Educational Research journal, 7: 477-492.

Wrightsman, L., Jr. (1962). The effects of anxiety, achievement motivation, and task importance upon performance on an intelligence test. Journal of Educational Psychology, 53: 150-156.

Yamamoto, K. and Dizney, H. (1965). Effects of three sets of test instructions on scores on an intelligence scale. Educational and Psychological Measurement, 25: 87-94.

Yelon, S. and Schmidt, W. (1971). The effect of objectives and instructions on the learning of a complex cognitive task. Paper presented at the annual meeting of the American Educational Research Association, New York.

Yinger, R. (1977). A study of teacher planning: Description and theory development ethnographic and information processing methods. Unpublished doctoral dissertation, Michigan State University.

Zahorik, J. (1968). Classroom feedback behavior of teachers. The Journal of Educational Research, 62: 147-150.

Zahorik, J. (1975). Teachers' planning models. Paper presented at the meetings of the American Educational Research Association, Washington, D.C.

Zahorik, J. (1970). The effect of planning on teaching. The Elementary School Journal, 3: 143-151.

Zatz, S. and Chassin, L. (1985). Cognitions of test-anxious children under naturalistic test-taking conditions. Journal of Consulting and Clinical Psychology, 53(3): 393-401.

Zeidner, M. and Safir, M. (1989). Sex, ethnic, and social differences in test anxiety among Israeli adolescents. Journal of Genetic Psychology, 150(2): 175-185.

About the Author

Joseph Wise served as Superintendent of Schools for Duval County (Jacksonville, FL) Public Schools and as Superintendent of Schools for Christina School District in Wilmington, Delaware. In Duval, Wise led the academic plans and programs and directed all strategic efforts for the district's 160+ schools, 126,000 students, and 14,000 employees.

Dr. Wise also served as Chief Education Officer with Edison Learning, which provides programs and services for 340,000 in 25 US states and in the UK. Wise continues as Managing Director and chief researcher for Atlantic Research Partners. Dr. Wise began his teaching career as a teacher in Georgia public schools and later joined the Orange County (FL) schools where he served in numerous leadership capacities. In addition, he worked in executive leadership positions in Anne Arundel County Public Schools (MD) Charlotte-Mecklenburg Public Schools (NC), The Walt Disney Company, and eSchool Solutions, Inc., a technology firm where he served as Chairman and Chief Executive Officer.

Dr. Wise has earned numerous honors including being named the 2006 Champion for Children, a national award presented by the HOSTS Learning organization. In addition, Wise was appointed to the National Commission on Writing for America's Families, Schools, and Colleges, selected by the Eli Broad Institute for School Boards as a Broad Fellow (2005), appointed to the Eli Broad Urban Superintendents Academy as a Fellow (2003), and recruited to the academy's adjunct faculty and advisory committee. Dr. Wise also serves on the Board of Directors for the Northwest Evaluation Association, a non-profit assessment firm that supports teaching and learning for more than 4 million students in more than 3,000 U.S. school districts.

In addition to his professional achievements, Dr. Wise has an extensive list of personal and community service awards including a lifetime membership with the NAACP, lifetime membership in the Florida Association of PTAs, and a founding member of the District Management Council.

Dr. Wise holds a doctorate from the University of Florida, a master's degree from the University of Central Florida, and a bachelor's degree from Florida State University.

About the Editor and Co-Author

David Sundstrom served as Chief of Staff for Duval County Public Schools (our Nation's 20th largest urban school district) and previously as Chief of Staff for the Christina School District in Wilmington DE. Sundstrom also served as Vice President for Organizational Development and Employee Relations for Edison Learning, and continues as Chairman and Managing Partner of *Atlantic Research Partners*—a firm dedicated to supporting high potential leaders in important organizations.

Sundstrom is an attorney who, before attending law school, was an elementary school teacher in rural Parkers Corners, Michigan. Additionally, he taught at Michigan State University for more than nine years, with a focus on senior-level courses in both commercial transactions and business law in the University's Business Law and Finance Departments. In 1995, Sundstrom also began teaching courses in *Trial Advocacy, Advanced Legal Writing,* and *Law Practice* at the Thomas M. Cooley Law School in Lansing, Michigan. Dr. Sundstrom further served as a full-time constitutional and legal advisor to the state of Michigan's Legislature from 1990 to 1999, with a focus primarily on labor and civil rights legislation.

Sundstrom began practicing law at the Detroit firm of *Gandelot, Stoepker and Dickson* in 1985; although his primary practice initially focused on civil litigation, Sundstrom also designed and implemented employment protocols and guidelines for a number of the firm's corporate clients. During his years in private practice, he also litigated cases arising from contractual and labor disputes, and further successfully served as trial counsel in both federal and state court cases involving employment and civil rights issues.

Before returning to preK-12 education, Sundstrom served as legal counsel and Chief Corporate Officer for the third largest provider of administrative software products and services to the North American preK-12 educational market.

Sundstrom is licensed to practice law in both Michigan and Florida.

I am the most fortunate of men for I am eternal.
Others live in the world today. I live in the world of tomorrow.
Others find purpose in the transient and the temporal;
I find meaning in the enduring and the eternal.

For I am charged with that most sacred mission—to transmit all that
our forebears lived for, loved for, and died for to the next
generation.

I span the generations—making the wisdom of the past live now
so that the future will have meaning.

I make wisdom live, for I am a bearer of knowledge.
I do not simply teach the mind.
I reach the heart, and when I reach the heart
I touch the soul.

To those who say two generations hence, what will I be,
if not a distant memory?

I respond: Though the mind fades, memories linger.
Though the body fails, the spirit prevails.
Though the scroll burns, the letters dance in the air.

--Rabbi Zev Schostak
on
the power of Teachers to change lives